Becoming Happy: 30 Ways to Heal Your Mind, Body and Soul

Kim Somers Egelsee

Cover Design by Kim Somers Egelsee

Victory Publishing
Casper, Wy
Publications printed in the United States

Table of Contents

"Becoming Happy - 30 Ways to Heal Your Mind, Body & Soul is a transformative guide that's for anyone seeking to bring more joy, balance, and healing into their lives. In bringing together this inspirational group of authors, Kim Somers Egelsee masterfully combines personal insights and practical tools, making this book an inspiring and essential read for anyone on a journey to greater happiness."
>-Monick Halm: Speaker/ Founder of Real Estate Investor Goddesses

"Such a divinely timed book that speaks to so many aspects of a persons entire being through the wide lens of varied perspectives. The ability to see from another perspective is such a healing and freeing tool in and of itself, and this compilation of inspirational insights and truths, intelligently delivered, reaches to the core of anyone guided to receive this wisdom."
>- Iseluleko (Kiko Ellsworth) Keynote Speaker | Male Coach | Emmy Award Winning Actor

Long time friend Kim Somers Egelsee has put together many powerful insights and strategies on how you can cultivate self-love daily to show up best for yourself and others. Kim and her authors will encourage and inspire you to become your best self!
>-Kyle Wilson, Founder Jim Rohn Int and KyleWilson.com, Strategist, Speaker and 10x #1 Bestselling author

'In a world often clouded by chaos and uncertainty, the pursuit of happiness stands as a universal aspiration. Yet, amidst the noise and distractions of everyday life, it's so easy for us to overlook the fundamental connection between mental health and true happiness. "Becoming Happy" isn't just about fleeting moments of joy or external achievements; it's about cultivating a profound sense of well-being that stems from within.

Central to this journey of self-discovery and fulfillment is the acknowledgment that mental health is the cornerstone of our happiness and healing. Our minds, just like our bodies, require care, attention, and compassion to thrive. However, for too long, stigma and shame have shrouded discussions around mental health, preventing many from seeking the support and understanding they desperately need.

Yet, amidst the shadows, I will stand proud and say there is light.

It is in our collective stories of struggle, resilience, and triumph, just as you will read in this book, that we find the power to combat stigma and ignite hope.

Through our healing journeys and the courage to share our experiences, we not only break down barriers but also pave the way for others to seek help without fear or judgment.

This ripple effect of healing and storytelling extends far beyond individual lives, transcending borders and cultures to create a global movement for change. It is within this movement that a mission that was placed on my heart, the Imperfectly Perfect Campaign found its purpose—to be a beacon of solidarity and advocacy dedicated to reshaping the narrative around mental health globally.

Through its collective efforts and my unwavering commitment, the Imperfectly Perfect Campaign empowers individuals worldwide to embrace their vulnerabilities, celebrate their strengths, and advocate for a world where mental health is treated with the same reverence as physical health. It is a testament to the transformative power of community, reminding us that together, we have the capacity to create profound change, one story at a time.

As you embark on your own journey towards becoming happy, remember that healing is not a solitary pursuit but a shared endeavor.

May the voices, the experiences, and the collective resilience you will read by the incredible co-authors in this book serve as beacons of hope, guiding you towards the light of understanding and acceptance for yourself.'

Glenn Marsden

Founder | Speaker | Thought Leader

imperfectlyperfectcampaign.org | glennmarsden.com

This book is dedicated to my amazing parents, Mike and Nancy Somers, who are the best parents and friends and taught me how to be a great Mom.

Introduction

I'm Kim Somers Egelsee, and I am a wife (happily married for over 25 years) and mom of two girls, a life and business coach, intuitive, #1 best-selling author, TEDx speaker, and podcast host. I love helping people step into confidence, increase self-love, know themselves deeply, and tune into their own inner power and higher self. I've spent the last thirty years studying personal, business, and spiritual teachings.

This book came about because of my meditating and channeling in the title and information about how it would come to fruition, and "Becoming Happy: 30 Ways to Heal Your Mind, Body and Soul" was born. I was so excited and being a person who jumps right in when inspired, I got to work. This book is so important because only about 14% of adults say that they're very happy, and most of the time, it's due to a lack of tools in knowing how to heal and learn how to be happy.

This life-changing book is a guide for men and women to transform their lives through reading stories with real-life examples of becoming happy. It will be a go-to guide to support, uplift, and encourage people so that they do not feel alone in their journey, and for them to become inspired to heal their mind, body, and soul. This book is for you if you want to increase your happiness physically, mentally, and emotionally.

A big reason this book resonated with me was my upbringing. I want to credit my parents as being a gigantic reason I have looked to the positive, the peaceful, and the optimistic side of life. Raised as an only child, I spent a lot of time with them and really felt, and still do today, that they were my parents and my friends. They always had me looking at the bright side of problems or challenges, believed in me and taught me to believe in myself, and focused on the love of life. We have always had fun adventures planned such as travel, concerts, shows, and family time connecting. It kept me in awe, almost always able to find something happy or grateful in each experience or situation. To this day we still do those things together and I am kept in amazement of the wonders of the world.

However, like most humans, I have had immense ups and light-filled times and some very dark and difficult downs. I have found that the choices you make are a very quintessential, if not the most important, part of living a healthy and happy life filled with love, peace, joy, and balance. Here is one way to become happier.

There were times in my past when I was younger, when I would make choices based on mere status, excitement, rebellion, ego or just trying to escape. To illustrate, things like choosing the good-looking popular guy to date, even though he was a jerk and a liar, going to certain prestigious events and parties just to be able to tell people that I went and to say I was there. I went through some bullying at school and experienced being abandoned by kids in the neighborhood as a child, as a result spent many years trying to people please and say yes to hanging out with anyone and everyone just to make sure I had enough friends in my life. I had no boundaries and would engage in trivial behavior: doing stupid things like ditching school at age 14 and getting caught, throwing a wild party at my parent's house when they were out of town where valuable things were stolen, just to be cool and accepted. These were all part of my life choices, and as a result, I was left with guilt, feeling like I was betraying myself, and just feeling low. This was not happy. I learned the hard way that the choices you make have a direct effect, connection, and influence on your happiness. This includes the people which you hang around, what you do with your time, where you go, what you think about, and even what you put into your body- all have the power to make or break happiness.

After researching confidence, positivity, happiness, and communication for years, getting my bachelor's degree in communication, and my credentials in educational psychology, which studies personal, moral, and social development, I developed a confidence course and life coach certification course, and created a life-changing method around choices. Now, for many years, I've had feedback from hundreds of people who have used this method in creating and choosing happiness in their lives, which adds peace, freedom, and being true to oneself and thus aids in healing the mind, body, and soul.

Choices are so essential to being true to you! When you are true to yourself, you are being honest with what you feel: your own desires, wants, needs, and in alignment with who you are. Choosing an alignment to self is when you completely accept yourself as the one who is in control of your own heart and feelings. You can also be tuned into your higher self. Tapping into your higher self allows you to embrace each moment fully and appreciate it for what it is. Spirituality is a key factor in allowing you to connect to your conscious guide - your higher Self. It is the constant connection to God or divine energy. I like the technique of tuning into the top of my head (crown chakra) and my heart, and the heavens. This gives you even more positive power, clarity, and insights in making the right choices for you.

The method to make positive choices that I created is called the 0-100 method. Every 2-3 months, make a list with two columns. In column one, write down everything you are doing now in your life: this includes your job tasks, habits, who you are helping or spending time with, hobbies, social activities, wellness, and more. In the second column, write down all of the visions, dreams, and goals you'd like to have happen in the next few years. Next, rate each item 0-100%: 100 being that it makes you feel alive, it is aligned with you, and it feels right in your heart and soul. If you rate something 50 or 60, it isn't great, and 30 or less would be very low, meaning it doesn't match or resonate with you. Finally, get rid of or lessen the things on the list that aren't at least 90% or even better, 100 percent, to make the space for greatness, rewards, and your dreams to come into your life.

Next, start to shape and sculpt your life by design. What about the things you are currently doing can you be better at? What are your dreams, and are you on your way to them? Notice how your choices are what make life interesting, adventurous, meaningful, and happy.
This is just one way to be happy and healthy, among thirty more written about in this magical book.
Enjoy!

Kim Somers Egelsee
#1 best-selling author, life and business coach, intuitive, podcast host, and TEDx speaker
www.kimlifecoach.com

Chapter 1

I'm Dianne. I'm a best-selling author, speaker, coach, radio show host, and philanthropist. I'm also a tough warrior, and lover of deep conversations, beautiful nature, dressing joyfully, and being a grandmother. I am passionate about encouraging people to embrace gratitude and live urgently.

The Practice of Happiness

"Fat cow."

"I'm embarrassed to be seen with you."

"Don't worry about the interview – they don't hire fat people for a job like that."

"No man wants a woman who looks like you."

My husband's cruel words were going through my brain on that sunny Sunday afternoon as I stood in front of my bathroom mirror, the door locked, holding a gun to my head.

I was at rock bottom, completely broken. After years of hearing this ugliness from the person who had promised to love me, my senses of happiness, confidence, and self-worth were laying in shards around my feet.

"Just pull the trigger," my broken heart whispered, "it will serve him right."

Thank God a different voice quietly spoke up, saying, "But what will this do to your parents? Your friends? Your family?"

I set the gun down.

I'd love to tell you that I packed a bag and walked out on my marriage that afternoon, but I can't. It took a few more years of conscious work to begin reclaiming my happiness, confidence, and self-worth.

It's been almost 25 years since that awful afternoon. Since then, I've focused on improving my self-talk, researching happiness and confidence, changing my soul nutrition, and PRACTICING being happy.

I moved back to my hometown to be closer to my family, got that divorce, met and married a loving and wonderful man, helped him finish raising his daughter and son, and became a 4-time cancer survivor – three life-threatening fights with blood cancer and one with breast cancer.

Sitting in my surgeon's office early in 2022, I learned I was not a candidate for reconstruction after my double mastectomy. I was about to lose my beautiful 44DD breasts and would not be able to replace them with the perky versions I envisioned. Those girls had been part of my identity for my whole adult life, and it was a shock to imagine my new reality.

My surgeon suggested a support group to help rebuild my self-esteem and confidence. My next words surprised me but made me realize how much I had grown. Taking a deep breath, I said, "Nope. I don't need breasts to feel like a confident woman. I'm going to be great."

And I am great, happy, confident, and certain of my value as a woman and a human. That day I experienced a sense that my years of deep inner work had worked.

Here's what I know – if I can reclaim my happiness, confidence, and self-worth, you can too. Looking back, I see I did it in three overlapping stages: Choose Happiness, Practice Happiness, and Share Happiness.

Choose Happiness

It sounds easy, doesn't it? There are a lot of social media posts and memes that make it sound like a breeze to just *be happy*. I admit that I share some of them on my social media. Why? Not to make people feel bad for feeling bad but to remind them of their power to choose.

To choose to pursue happiness (and confidence and self-worth), you first must believe that these ways of being are possible. Not just for some lucky people, but for YOU, the complex, pessimistic, struggling YOU.

You have so much more power than you might think. You have ALL the power because no one can take up space in your head and heart unless you let them. You are the controller of the volume dial; turn up the good, mute the bad, and delete the ugly.

You have to accept that you have that power and then CHOOSE to use it. For years, I have said, sometimes quietly in my head, sometimes out loud – "NO." I do this when negative thoughts, harsh memories, or the mean talk greatest hits slide into my brain and try to take me down.

Choose to stop that negative self-talk, and day by day, you make room for the happiness and confidence you were born to have. This one choice will change your life. It changed mine.

Practice Happiness

Happiness is a practice. It's the thoughts, activities, and behaviors you **choose** each day. What is happiness to you? What makes you feel joyful, confident, and worthy? How can you get more of those things into your life?

A word here: happiness is always an inside job. When you think of what happiness is to you, you do not give any person, thing, or experience the power to make you happy or UNhappy. Yes, marriage and family, sports cars, and tropical vacations are wonderful, but plenty of people who have those things are still heartbreakingly unhappy. I learned that your happiness is found and nurtured inside of you.

One of the things I've been doing for the past 25 years in my practice of happiness is monitoring my soul nutrition. Instead of filling my head and heart with junk food like true-crime books, doom and gloom news, and mean-spirited people (online and in real life), I choose to bring lightheartedness into my daily life.

I've curated my social media feeds to show me yummy recipes, inspiring thoughts, and photos of baby animals. I've edited my calendar to make time for people and projects that bring energy and joy into my life, not deplete them. I've programmed my Kindle and streaming accounts with books and movies that are funny, thought-provoking, and inspiring.

Living in happiness and confidence is something you intentionally practice every day through your thoughts, behaviors, and activities. I've found that there is no graduation for this deeply personal work: no diploma or certificate – but there **are** milestones like that day in my surgeon's office along the way.

Share Happiness

My favorite part of practicing happiness is sharing my happiness with others. I read somewhere that happiness shared is happiness doubled. I know this to be true.

There are literally thousands of ways to share happiness. You might discipline yourself to talk less about the bad things in your life and focus more on the good. You might share funny or inspirational posts on your social media. One of my favorite things is complimenting people – friends and strangers. You might make someone's day with your kind words. You will also make your own day. See? Double the happiness.

I encourage you to look for ways to share some happy moments with others. It reminds you that happiness exists in the world and confirms that you are meant to live in happiness, too.

Dianne Callahan can be found at www.CatalystCoaching.biz for coaching and speaking inquiries. For joyful inspiration and connection, join Dianne's Lighthearted Life Community on Facebook.

Chapter 2
"Hidden Gifts"

I'm Lisa, a warm passionate, and caring lover of travel, nature, and animals. I am also a mom, wife, an intuitive and creative entrepreneur. People would say I am a positive and joyful person, and I would like to say that I have chosen to be. I have also experienced the opposite: trauma, sadness, pain, etc. as most of us have at one point in time and it is not a fun place to be. We all have coping mechanisms that get us out of sadness or a funk.

Becoming happy is one thing, staying happy is another. Our bodies, minds, and souls are constantly in flux, ever moving, and usually never in sync. Why is that? When the soul creates the path, the mind must remain consistent, and then the body must follow. I always believed that positivity and joy are a choice, and you must choose to work at it once you get there.

My choice to become and stay joyful came from faith and my faith came from knowing there is a higher power and that high power, whatever it might be wants us to be joyful.

This higher power supports us by connecting and extending our energy field to those around us. And if you are sensitive, you can feel that energy and feel whether the person around you feels "positive" or "negative." Combining that with the law of attraction, you create your own circumstances and experiences from then on.

When you move through these "experiences" you observe subtleties in ways of how you see (Mind), feel, (Body), or know (Soul) about these experiences. I learned from an early age that I experienced certain senses in a stronger more dynamic way. Seeing in my mind pictures and stories, not unlike a movie would play through my mind gave me a firsthand view of something that was to become, or something was directly in front of me. Sometimes in conjunction with this, I would "hear" a voice or words describing and a "feeling" of how the situation would play out. I would seek out books that gave me a greater understanding of what I was experiencing and how they affected me. My conclusion was that I was not only clairvoyant but clairsentient, clairaudient, and claircognizant. These are gifts we all possess, I just found out at an earlier age what this was and began to utilize it in my everyday interactions. Eventually, this new way of being was the tool I used for self-reliance, positivity faith, and creativity— my foundation for being joyful.

This was not an easy acceptance early on of these "hidden gifts" and for most of my life, I hid them from people, which was hard because I was a bit sassy and mouthy. My early experience was announcing that someone was going to get divorced, and at six years old that was not a joyful or positive thing to announce to a bunch of adults, especially when nobody knew, not sure if the couple even knew yet. Or the time I described my best friend's husband who she had not met yet down to the physical description. That was received more positively. Or, seeing a picture in my mind of a friend's dear friend together as they were dressed in costumes which that had worn together and describing the photo in detail to my friend providing her with comfort that her friend was in a peaceful happy place after she passed on. These joyful visions gave hope and faith to people I connected with and in turn created more joy in my life as I felt I was giving gifts to those who needed them.

So, how do we tap into these "special gifts" we all possess to aid us in feeling joyful? Practice until it flows through you as a natural state. I have a few exercises I teach it my Intuitive eye-visualization (Do you see the answer in word, symbol, or picture form) Clairvoyant or clear seeing.

Intuitive ear- (Can you hear the answer? Hear a word, phrase, or statement?) Clairaudience or clear hearing.

Intuitive feel- heart (Can you connect and interpret others' emotions? Can you tap into this for greater empathetic accuracy?) Clair sentient or clear feeling

Intuitive know–gut (Do you have a gut reaction to a specific situation, problem, or circumstance?) Clear knowing or claircognizant. Below is a fun simple exercise to get you started.

-Your Intuitive Eye- Emphasis on Radiating Positivity and Joy

Sit quietly

Relax your eyebrows and forehead.

Let the muscles of your face 'melt' into ease.

Inhale and exhale rhythmically.

With your inner eyes, create a vision of you radiating health and happiness to every part of your body and all those around you.

So, in essence, anything we do that we want to become good at we have to practice, which is the same for our mindset. We choose how we want to feel and what we want to become, and this takes practice, It's the essence of positivity and joy. When we are positive, we exude a joyful vibration that extends to others and then hopefully it is received and expanded further into a collective humanity.

Lisa Huscher

Using your "Hidden Gifts" to create positivity and joy in yourself and those around you.

Intuitive/Author/Speaker/Co-Founder of High Vibe Soul Sisters

www.TheSoulsGifts.com

Chapter 3
It's The Yoga

Somewhat unwittingly, this has become my tagline, my mantra, and my motto: it's the yoga.

It began in a comedic moment my mom retold to me after she was in labor and delivery with me, my husband at the time, and our team of nurses, as I gave birth to our first child, our daughter, about 25 years ago.

I was in my first-year long yoga teacher training program when we discovered I was pregnant. Fortunately, we felt ready as a newly married couple, and I was deep in my learning, and early practices of yoga, so, it was perfect then to let that be part of my prenatal prep and wellness.

In labor and delivery, during a slow moment, after some intense pushing for hours due to a posterior position fetus– as my mom retold it, the nurses commented on and even complimented me about how calm and composed I was to be through the potentially difficult labor. I guess I looked at them, smiled, and said, "it's the yoga" in a wo-an-in labor kind of voice, of course! I laughed at this and retold it over the years, but it also became this undeniably accurate statement and response to other observations I've received over the years.

You look so young.
Thanks, "it's the yoga".

You always seem so present and relaxed. Thanks, "it's the yoga".

Wow, you always have a lot of energy!
"It's the yoga".

I love how you are so friendly and seem to love people.
Thanks. Need I say it? "It's the yoga".

How can "the yoga" be responsible, or deserve credit for all of these favorable perceptions of me in the world? And do I mean the exercises of yoga?
Well, yes, and no. I do fit in daily, personalized use of specific exercises/poses/stretches that take care of my posture, agility, my nervous system, and my physiological well-being.

I am also more aware than ever that this daily use of movement and breath as medicine is also absolutely energy work that I am doing with myself each day. Yoga and science teach that we are energetic beings, and it is all energy: including all aspects of body, mind, mood, mental health, and emotions. So, our daily use of even the most gentle, simple stretches, does aid us greatly in facilitating awesome health and vitality, as well as supporting us in better feeling mood, attitude, and mindset, quite naturally.

But one of the biggest lessons I have been sharing in my now 25 years of teaching, speaking, and writing about yoga, meditation, and mindfulness is that the word yoga just means union. Yoga actually can be anything that helps grow our feelings of union, connection, and oneness with ourselves in body and mind, as well as a sense of connection to others and feelings of spiritual connection–within and around us. Anything that facilitates our yoga/ union at this moment, in a sense of mindfulness, which is part of what yoga teaches primarily, is this presence as part of the system of psychology that yoga can bring. It is definitely in our use and cultivation of our attention, mind power, and state of being. This is yoga.

This may look different for each of us. The more personal you get with what "tunes you" as I like to say and helps to you feel more connected is part of what you can build in and how you can use yoga for yourself in your practices.

Yes, yoga teaches that daily practice is an ideal way to cultivate habituated ways of taking care of ourselves, in our full range of being, and yes, experiencing happiness.

Yoga also teaches that we do have this natural flow and connection within us to spirit/God, Lifeforce, and Shakti – which can be experienced as happiness, love, joy, and even ecstasy.

Yoga opens us to the awareness that many of us have stored memories and emotions of the past, which we now call words like trauma, that can become a block to our Shakti energy and our connection to that natural state of happiness, love, and God within us.

Beautifully, our practices of yoga are intended to be a place and a chance to do that inner work to feel, release and transform these energy blockages, called samskaras, in yoga. As we continue to remove and release these energies that block our connection, we ne to tap into that natural happiness that yogis propose exists within all of us. I love that perspective.

Now, I see more than ever that it's the yoga in our varied and expanding practices, perspectives, and psychology that can absolutely be a system to becoming happy and staying more in our happy, for the rest of our precious lives. By implementing systematic self-care to tune us into our spirituality, we can reconnect with the happiness within us.

I hope this has been helpful to you along your journey of creating and cultivating your sense of happiness. If I can be of help to you in developing your personal, daily practices of self-care and spirituality, please reach out for one on one/group programs and or check out my podcast, social media and books.

Laura Jane – LJ
@tuneyouwithlj

Chapter 4
Gratitude

I always seemed to secure employment in the public sector. It fits me well since I like serving people. As a young girl, I had no idea I would become a School Counselor and most recently a published author. Participating in *this book* seemed like a good next step. Looking back at my life I could see how events have led me to realize the blessings I was afforded. I am thankful for the ups, downs, twists, and turns. Amid it all, I could see how gratitude has helped shape my life. Recently I authored a book entitled Moments a Guided Gratitude Journal about my fun, amazing, and miraculous experiences. In summary, I have lived a life of *gratitude*.

When I was around eight years old, a car almost hit me; I was crossing a highly traveled street. I have never forgotten the incident because it was scary. Thankfully, nothing happened. I am grateful.

One time my mom and her best friend drove me to college to get me enrolled. We did not have money for me to go to college. We drove there anyway. I stood in the shadows watching as my mom had a discussion with the lady in charge of the money. All I could think was, I cannot afford college.

After a long time of waiting, my mom turned to me after she had finished the deal. She had enrolled her daughter in college! How did she do that? You can go to college and not pay? It all made sense later in life when I received notices about school loans.

It was an enjoyable time and a wonderful experience. I have great memories. I stay connected with friends. Because of this, I am grateful.

Four years later. I packed up my apartment and bought a one-way plane ticket to my next destination. I decided to try something new. College did not teach me about what to do upon graduation. But I had a plan: Go to a city I had never traveled to thousands of miles away and meet relatives I had never seen. With a carry-on bag, a trunk, a one-way ticket, and $15, I arrived in paradise.

I am in awe of how I blindly but bravely took that big step. I was a quiet and shy person who did not think outside of the box. Deciding to try something out of my wheelhouse was exciting and for that I am grateful.

An experience I had as a young adult, did not bring me joy. One evening I recall being sleepy at work. I anticipated getting off that swing shift and rushing home. I fell asleep and rolled my car down an off ramp. The car landed right side up. I kicked the door open and ran up the off ramp in the direction of the sound from cars passing by.

Some disappointments that evolved from this event. But I am happy I had no broken bones and no bloodshed. I did go to the chiropractor and physical therapy. Now, when I pass someone on the freeway who has been in an accident, I will silently pray for him or her on the spot.

One time, I traveled to Europe to visit a friend. When I got there the first thing she told me after hugs and hellos was, "I have to work this week." I thought, about what I would do. I pulled up my big girl pants and went for it. I got up every morning, dressed, and went to the kiosk to purchase a ticket into town. I stopped in a coffee shop; window-shopped, visited a museum, and took pictures. I found a little church to attend later that night. I went home, told my friend about it, and went back that night. I met friends at church. They gave me a ride home. I had a broad experience, and I am grateful for that trip.

Now that I have shared what being grateful looks like to me, what can you do to begin incorporating gratitude into your life?

I first heard about the benefit of practicing gratitude years ago from the talk show host, Oprah Winfrey. She encouraged everyone *"to write five things we are grateful for every day."* I began doing it. Also, Dr. Joe Dispenza said, "*You strengthen your immune system when you practice gratitude."* He said, "It is going to be something that you want to do all the time."

Practicing gratitude is what I depend on as a daily regimen. During the last few years dating back to 2020 when the world experienced unusual and unique events, sometimes it was tough to just breathe. I am speaking for myself as well as others. In the type of work, I do I interact with people who experience high anxiety. I started a **gratitude journal club** with a group of people to help us get through a tough time.

Look around you. Think about anything positive you notice. *"Put a smile on your face and say, thank you."* Take it a step further and **feel the positivity.** Maintain a **healthy environment.** It matters who you hang out with and the spaces you find yourself in. I heard it takes fewer muscles to **smile** than it is to frown. I always feel better when I am smiling. You will as well.

If showing gratitude seems to be a challenge for you, know that what you are going through may not compare to what someone else is going through. That job you may not like is a job someone else would be happy to have. Those kids who give you grief, someone who is childless wishes they had children. That ten-year-old car you wish you could upgrade, someone at the bus stop would trade their bus pass for it.

What do you like to do? *Find something to do. Have a hobby. Enjoy life!* It is not up to anyone else but you. *Jot down notes about something that you are grateful about*. Put them in a box or a jar. One in a while go back and read what you are grateful for and *reflect on the blessings* you experienced. Start your gratitude journey today!
Debbie Dee Hornaday
School Counselor/Author
To get a copy my book; https://tinyurl.com/29r2f37u

Chapter 5
Getting to Know and Love the True You

I'm the most social, person I know, who loves to be alone. I'm Casey Krebs, an avid learner and teacher.

I love learning and miss it when I don't have something new in my life to learn.
I studied for 4 years in university and went on to earn my Master's Degree in education. I've completed baking courses at Le Cordon Bleu, a Master Gardener certification, and I'm a certified dog handler with St. John's Ambulance Therapy Dogs. I make kombucha, yogurt, dry herbs, and roast coffee beans. I try to make everything from scratch in my home from ketchup to bone broth to my dog's dinner. I'm an artist, baker, traveler, adventurer, entrepreneur, and math lover. I love reading and will learn everything I can about a topic. I deep dive into learning and give back that knowledge when I can, by teaching. When I've pulled away from teaching in the past, it has always called me back, and eventually I answer. I've taught entrepreneurs how to start businesses, taught baking and cooking workshops, language, calculus, non-toxic living, and gardening. I love all of it. Though it took space, quiet and reflection to get here.

Growing up in a household of 10 people, alone time was rare. If my parents went out, I'd sprint to their bedroom, a sister on my heels ready to lock myself in to watch television. Alone. At 9 years old I begged my parents to send me to overnight camp. I was young but they finally agreed. When they asked me who I wanted to go with, I didn't understand the question, nor the surprised look on their face when I said no one. I'll go by myself. In school, I'd find time and space to look out the window and think. I'd daydream: about what I now know to be meditation. I'd dive deep into my imagination, thoughts, and sometimes nothing.

At 18 I went off to university, even though I had a loving family to stay home with and a college nearby. I craved the independent adventure and left everything I knew to study and live on campus. In my early 20s I left my dream job, and my family to move to a bigger dream job of living in Malibu. I was once again craving adventure, and going solo didn't even enter my mind as a concern.

In March 2020 when life shifted and everything slowed down and shut down, I dug my heels in deep. No trade shows, networking meetings, dinners out with 'acquaintances'. There was nothing to do but "be". It was a new world, and I embraced the slowness and delved into what I really liked to do. I soon realized that I didn't enjoy all the meetings and busyness that I was creating for myself.

I loved my new free time and, in turn, found what really filled me up. My life became methodical, deliberate, and intentional. I melted into the slow steps and melodic rhythm of my new world and walked in sync with its meditative pace. I was drawn to slow living in food and nature and delved deep into an intricate and patient lifestyle. I was baking, mushroom foraging, cheese making, fermenting, cooking, gardening, hiking, and seed saving.

When things started opening up again, I found myself saying no to everything. I did not want to have another booth at a trade show or go to a networking event in my industry. I decided to consciously keep my slow pace. I desired to be with my family, close friends, and anything that brought me joy, meaning, and fulfillment. I allowed my calendar to be blank for a year.

For the first time in a long time, I found art again. I had time to crack open my box of childhood keepsakes and read past stories and report cards. I noticed a theme emerging amongst my teachers who discussed my creativity, love of writing, storytelling, and art. I started to explore and re-discover my artistic side just as I moved to an incredible artist community. I explored oil painting, and glasswork, and deep dove into ceramics among other mediums. In this season, I became slow, meaningful, purposeful, and filled with joy. I went into hibernation with my family and now I'm in a balance. I still pick and choose very deliberately how I spend my time and with whom. And sometimes, I prefer to go places alone so I can fully immerse myself in the experience.

When you slow down, you can see who you are and what really serves you. Sometimes you don't realize who you are, have become, or who you need or want to be until you slow down, and examine your inner self. You may be currently misaligned with your true self, which could lead to feelings of disconnect. Embrace your change. Go slow. Be mindful and present. Cut out the noise from your life and concentrate on your root, your core.

Sit down in a quiet space and choose what you want to do, what serves your inner being, your inner child, or your inner adult? Take time to listen to your heart. Go somewhere alone. Start with a hike, a stroll at the market, or a walk on the beach; once you make the time to slow down, your mind will have space to think, and create a way to streamline your world in a simple, wonderful way. Surround yourself with what matters and eliminate things that don't. Curate the life you want!

I remember vividly that 9-ye-r old wanting to go alone. I didn't want another person dictating or influencing my experience or creating a bubble in which I could feel coaxed to stay inside. A new adventure awaited: making friends, learning, exploring, experiencing, and having fun in a way that served me mattered. To do that I needed to have space, to be me. Being alone is different than being lonely. It's hanging out with your soul.

Written by Casey Krebs

Instagram @caseykrebs
Instagram @ayearofhappinaessandmeaning
Website caseykrebs.com

Chapter 6
A Dream of Roses

Hi, I am Shajen (Cheyenne) Joy Aziz, M.Ed., M.A. Author and co-creator of the international bestseller, movie, and documentary, Discover the Gift. I am a woman here to help others lean into their gifts and passions and heal their pain.

"Dream of Roses, Honey, and I will see you in the morning." Burning to the ground, life as I knew it would never be the same at the age of twelve. The house was gone; it was almost unfathomable that our home was no longer in existence. But alas, things would be okay. Mom, Demian, and I would begin again in a town familiar and comfortable. The Oasis, the only health food store, and café in our tri-state area, was owned by my mother. Things would be fine. Staying with close friends, one blanket at a time – we began to rebuild our lives.

While at a friend's house, I called my mother and told her I was sad and afraid of what was to come; she said, "Don't worry, everything is going to be ok, dream of roses, honey, and I'll see you in the morning." A dream unrealized as the roses turned into a nightmare; my mom, Fonda Joy Segal, died in a car accident that night. Scared, anxious, and frightened were the only things on the agenda, and funeral flowers would be the next bouquet I would receive.

Our charred belongings, other people's clothing, and the memories I hold dear became all I had left of what I knew to be solid and honest in my life. The physical sensations of grief catapulted my confusion about myself and life even more. At the age of twelve, alone, with no mother and scared, my father gave me to a local farming family who wanted a live-in caretaker for their children and someone to help with house chores and the farm. Far away from my father and brother, who were in NYC, I began a new life's journey; having no idea who I was, I found solace in journaling, a place to talk with mom, and where I began asking myself hard questions. Who am I? What do I do now? Where should I live, how will I survive, and who will help me? My escape became my journal. The need to unearth the pain was more significant than anything else, and in this process, I began to discover a new way to relieve myself of the heaviness within. I could feel the separation from the anguish as I wrote. It was as if I had no choice but to express myself because anything short of that would feel like death all over again.

Spiraling back to the question of "Who am I?" The devastating loss of my life as I knew it at twelve was the pinnacle of my pain for many years. Until I learned to transmutate that pain into a gift; I stayed burdened. As the weight lifted, I began to live. Wondering how I survived those days, I realized it was through my ongoing journaling. This process created a place for self-expression, a private window into the soul of my pain; a place to expel it. Learning to understand my healing journey through this process, I began to accept myself and my existence. Looking at the row of journals on my bookshelf, I saw, that moving forward, I could continue to fill them with pain, or I could choose differently and begin to fill them with life, of living, of love, loss, and triumph, and at that moment while engulfed in the process of my journey of helping others and writing about it, I had space from pain, even if brief, it was joyous.

"Amidst the worldly comings and goings, observe how endings become beginnings." Tao Te Ching

Our adversities are the events and experiences that catapult and help us discover who we are at levels previously unseen and unknown to ourselves. Neale Donald Walsh discusses reaching beyond your comfort zone. When we have experiences outside of our "normal," these different stimuli generate new responses that mandate that we find a way to adapt, grow, and ultimately - evolve. And let me be clear, these experiences do not have to be adverse. Instead, you can create them by stepping into your power by following your passions and gifts. As Janet Attwood teaches in Discover the Gift, "Your passions and gifts are the breadcrumbs that lead you on the journey of a life you love."

We are all a work in progress, always. The more mindful you can be about supporting the ongoing development of your internal conversations and thoughts, the more peace you will experience in your moments.

Our character and beliefs show up when adversity strikes. The hardships I experienced early in life made me grow up quickly in some areas and be a late bloomer in others. I learned prematurely about the fragility of life and the impermanence of the sentient beings in my world. Without guidance, it took me longer to understand myself, to set boundaries, and to choose wisely. My experiences created a fierce and focused mama tiger in me, one that wants the best for all children, and I believe this comes through the education and transformation of the adults in the world. Through journaling and reflecting, I came to understand my experiences and the importance of self-actualization, and this became my gift to the world.

Unexpectedly, I was offered the possibility of a lifetime: to author a book proposal that needed to go to the London Book Fair in 16 days. This was now about writing professionally, how was I going to do this? How was I going to step into this new way? Would people care what I had to say? Does my voice matter in the world? My self-doubt and burning solar plexus were telling me to run. Then I remembered, to lean into that of which I am afraid and befriend my demons.

When I sat down to write my first published book, Discover the Gift, at first, I thought, "Oh no, what am I going to say? How do I do this? And then I remembered, writing saved me, and "the key to writing is writing, so just write Shajen, write." Once I took that one step, the fear that had been keeping me back for so long was relinquished. And suddenly, I was in this different place with myself, really living my gift, being who I am. What happened was that the authentic me showed up, and I am so grateful." Writing and researching became my new way of life. I used the tools which helped me heal to propel me professionally. This learning was a powerful lesson for life.

Being open and receptive to your insight gives you the power to ignite clear intentions because every choice and interaction has brought you to this moment. You see, much of what you desire is not "out there;" it is already within you. The road to your inner knowing lies in remembering the connection of your heart, mind, body, and spirit. Focused action creates transformation, when you are ready to do the work.

I now know that looking for the Gift in every situation eases anxiety and stress and creates possibilities beyond your wildest dreams – because what you focus on expands.

Shajen Joy Aziz, Med.,M.A.

www.livingcurriculum.com

Chapter 7
Finding Joy Through Faith: My Journey

My name is Alvire Colimon Paul. I was born into a bustling family in Saint Marc, Haiti, on June 14, 1939, as the fifth of ten children. My childhood home was always alive with the sounds and sights of family life. My parents were far from wealthy. We were very poor in material possessions, but they endowed us with rich lessons in resilience, faith, and the importance of family and community. These values, instilled early on, would guide me through life's myriad paths and help me find positivity and happiness.

Early Foundations

When I was 16 years old, I went to join a convent in Haiti. I didn't join because I felt a strong spiritual calling. I joined because I wanted a bed to sleep in and some privacy. We were 10 kids in a 3-bedroom house, and I was very tired of sleeping on the floor! Even though I went for this rather mercenary reason, I fell in love with being in the convent and being of service to God.

Nevertheless, it soon became clear that my vibrant energy and curiosity about the world were meant for a different path. The nuns, recognizing that I might find my calling elsewhere, advised me to explore life beyond the convent. Trusting their insight and embracing the uncertainty, I left, setting out on a journey that would expand my horizons far beyond what I had imagined. I went back to school to finish my education. I graduated with a certificate as a bilingual secretary - working in French and English.

Global Adventures

My first job after graduation was in Algeria, North Africa, as a bilingual administrative assistant, a role that introduced me to a kaleidoscope of cultures and experiences. My sister and brother-in-law were living in Algeria and they helped arrange the position for me. Living and working in Algeria not only challenged my adaptability but also deepened my faith as I navigated life in a vastly different environment from Haiti. After several enriching years, I had to move abruptly. During the coup in 1962, I risked my life and my liberty to protect my then-boss, the Dean of the School of Medicine. I stood in the doorway, preventing armed revolutionaries from entering, while he escaped out the back door.

After many hours of being questioned without even a glass of water, I was able to leave by promising one of the revolutionaries that I would go on a date with him. My brother-in-law, who had been waiting outside the police station for hours for me, whisked me away and arranged for me to leave the country that night with the Catholic church on a plane to Lyon, France. Though this episode was harrowing, I felt God's protection throughout. It was a miracle that not a hair on my head was harmed, and I was able to escape. Many could not say the same.

Living in Lyon added layers of sophistication and further diversity to my life experiences, enriching my understanding of the world and strengthening my spiritual resolve. In France, amidst historic landscapes and the hustle of city life, I continued to rely on my faith to anchor me. My belief in God provided a sense of continuity and comfort, guiding me through everyday challenges and cultural adjustments.

Love and Family

Eventually, I ended up in the United States, seeking to reconnect with my roots and start anew. I found a job as a bilingual secretary at a convent, blending my clerical skills and my spiritual background. It was there, settled into the rhythm of American life, that another girl living in the same convent invited me out dancing one evening. That night, I met Henri, a fellow Haitian, with a kind smile and a charismatic presence. Our shared experiences as Haitian immigrants and our deep faith sparked an immediate connection. Henri and I found ourselves drawn together by our common values and aspirations for the future.

During our courtship, we engaged in deep discussions about life, faith, and our dreams. It didn't take long for us to realize we were meant to journey through life together. Within 11 months, we were married, embarking on a partnership grounded in mutual respect and shared spiritual beliefs.

Facing Trials

Together, Henri and I welcomed four children into our lives. Each child brought immense joy and a new set of challenges, and we raised them in a home where love, faith, and the values of our Haitian heritage were central. Our faith was not just a private comfort but a vibrant part of our family life, shaping how we celebrated joys and faced challenges.

Through the many ups and downs over the decades, it was always a faith in God and seeing the hidden blessings behind everything that enabled me to always find peace and happiness.

The most significant trial we encountered was the illness and subsequent loss of our eldest son, Marc-Henri, to cancer when he was 50, leaving his wife and two young children. This devastating experience tested our faith more deeply than anything else had. During Marc's illness, our family drew closer together, leaning heavily on our belief in God's plan and the support of our friends. Despite the profound grief, I found solace in believing that Marc was now at peace and in a better place. This belief helped sustain me and my family, providing comfort and a way to cope with the immense loss.

Reflections on Faith and Happiness

Through all these experiences, my faith has been the cornerstone of my happiness. It has taught me that joy does not come from external circumstances but from a deep, internal peace with God's plan for my life. Each challenge and joy I have faced has reinforced this belief, shaping a life that, while not without its trials, is profoundly fulfilling.

Faith has also shown me the importance of community. In both times of joy and times of need, the support of family and friends has been invaluable. This communal aspect of my faith has not only helped me but also allowed me to give back, supporting others in their times of need, thereby multiplying the happiness and support within my community.

Three Tips for Happiness:

1. Embrace Change and Uncertainty: View unexpected changes as opportunities for growth. When faced with uncertainty, ask yourself, "What can I learn from this new situation?" Remember, some of life's most beautiful chapters may begin with moments of uncertainty.
2. Cultivate a Strong Spiritual Foundation: Develop a regular spiritual practice. Set aside time each day for prayer, meditation, or reflection to connect with your beliefs and find inner peace. Let your faith be a guiding light through both joyous and challenging times.
3. Build and Nurture Community: Invest in your relationships. Reach out to friends and family regularly and look for opportunities to support others. Remember that giving support can be as fulfilling as receiving it. In both times of joy and need, the support of family and friends is invaluable.

Conclusion

As I look back on the roads I've traveled — from Haiti to Africa, Europe, and beyond — I see a life richly woven with the threads of faith, love, and resilience. With a strong spiritual foundation, a willingness to embrace change, and a supportive community, we can find joy and peace even in life's most challenging moments.

As you reflect on your own path to happiness, remember that each experience, whether joyful or difficult, contributes to the beautiful tapestry of your life. May your journey, like mine, be filled with learning, love, and the deep, abiding joy that comes from a life lived with purpose and faith. Life is a complex tapestry of experiences; with faith, each thread, whether dark or light, contributes to the beauty of the whole.

Alvire Colimon Paul

Chapter 8
The Paradox of Happiness

This is dedicated to Mom, who died in 2022. Written in four sections, her presence is in every word, every sorrow, every happiness. Being part of this beautiful project brought an unexpected healing I didn't know I needed.

Here's to *'becoming happy.'*

Truth

"...some people think the truth is the worst thing that can happen. The truth is not the worst thing that can happen."
- Tony Hoagland

Tony's words are like a punch to the heart, the kind I willingly lean in for. I often call on his words and the words of other unforgettable poets and sages. As a poet and writer, myself, the following is *my truth,* and I hope you find it helpful while you're on the road to finding yours.

There are two questions I've been grappling with since being invited to be part of this project.

"Do you really have something to contribute?"

"Are you happy 'enough' to write about *'becoming happy'***?"**

I asked myself those two questions dozens of times and, as a result, wrote dozens of drafts of this chapter. That was until I finally relaxed, stopped hammering myself for perfection, and asked myself the questions again - honestly listening and honestly answering.

"Yes. I do. And YES! I am happy... ***enough.***"

Getting my ego-mind in check and shifting my expectations of this submission from significant to sincere was liberating. I realized the struggle wasn't writing about ***becoming happy*** but writing about *'not being happy.'* It's no wonder each new draft felt like *"blah, blah, blah."* I couldn't find the heart in it until I did. The truth I'd been avoiding saying found its way to the page and got me to the other side. You were right, Tony. *"The truth is not the worst thing that can happen,"* and this is mine.

I have a complicated relationship with happiness. I'm not *'not happy'*; I'm just not chasing it. I'm not even sure I'm craving it. I don't believe happiness lives in a vacuum. I think the beauty and power of becoming happy are enhanced by the truthful telling of very real moments, of sharing what makes us more alike than separate, of saying to another person, *"This is my pain, this is my sadness, this is where I hurt."* And by asking, *"Where do YOU hurt, feel sad, feel pain?"* This is not a morbid exercise. In those moments of radical compassion, magic can happen. A connection is made, sometimes a bond. It might last a moment, it might last a lifetime, but it's real, and it means everything. Together, we shatter the idea that you cannot be happy if you're feeling sad, and that's just not true. So, in that tender place, happiness can bloom in the same space as sorrow.

Death is not the enemy of life
Death is not the killer of joy

My mom died two years ago, almost to the day. I was there. It was inhumane, brutal, and unkind. As Dylan Thomas willed for his dying father when reflecting on the time of his death, my sweet mother did not *"go gentle into that goodnight."* *She* did *"rage rage against the dying of the light."* It was devastating and one of the most savage experiences I've ever had in my life.

I held my mom as she took her last breath. In her final moments, she was like a wild animal dying in my arms. A wailing came out of her, like a banshee, howling with pain. It was like nothing I'd ever known. She had a titanium mechanical heart valve, and when she stood close to me, I could hear it working. Tic. Tic. Tic. Between her cries, in those brief seconds of quiet, I could hear the ticking of her lion heart, slowing to a dull roar.

A chant bellowed from my aching body to hers,
"I love you, Mom.
I'm here. I'm right here."

In her last moments, fighting for breath, she said her final words to me;
"No, You're Not! You're not here!"

and she left.

Surrendering to what Mary Oliver calls the '*soft animal of our body*' her weight gave into my arms. She was now someplace else. She wasn't here, and I wasn't there. My breathing slowed in an unconscious effort to match her breathlessness. I laid her back against the pillows, her beautiful golden, her mouth slightly open, her lips changing hue. Gone.

As poet Rosemary Wahtola Trommer writes:
so we might walk more openly
into this world so rife with devastation
This world, so ripe with joy

I am grateful I was there.
I am happy I heard her final words.
I am rife with devastation and grief, still.
I am ripe with joy for this life, always.

Keep going.
You're closer than you think.

In early 2020, I was launching a new program. It was called BLOOM! Using gardening, planting, growing, blossoming, and 'Blooming' as metaphors, I designed prompts around this theme. I was not yet a gardener but was in love with the theme. Not wanting to dial this in, I got busy and started to explore and research. How to be a good gardener? What to plant? When to start? I was curious about everything, including what it meant to have a gardener's mindset. Some questions kept coming to mind. What happens to a seed once it's deep into the soil? Do seeds communicate? How do the roots know to grow down, and the shoots know to grow up, and how do they know which is which?

I read about some botanists who were wondering the same thing. They did a test by planting several seeds, then put impediments in their path to see how it affected their growth. They made the journey arduous for these little seeds using rocks and stones, bricks, and debris. Though the seeds were nourished, they'd have to find their way through the nearly impossible obstacles directly in their path. They were alive, but could they live?

Like little miracles, they forged ahead. They found their way. They pushed beyond the boundaries and were not deterred. The obstacles did not stop their growth. They course-corrected, took the long route where needed, and kept going.

I was in tears. What a beautiful thing, this story of triumph. This made me happy and brought me to this conclusion.

The seed is not confused by the darkness.

"I like living. I have sometimes been wildly, despairingly, acutely miserable, wracked with sorrow, but through it all, I still know quite certainly that just to be alive is a grand thing."
-   Agatha Christie

The legacy of death is life

Doesn't everything die at last, and too soon?
Tell me, what is it you plan to do
with your one wild and precious life?
-   Mary Oliver

The best gift we can give ourselves when time is running out is to live. To allow ourselves to be happy. Yes, it's fleeting and please, don't pretend it's not. Embrace and cherish and LIVE, your one wild and precious life.

It's okay to not be okay, and it's okay to laugh when we're sad, to sing when our hearts are breaking, and to let in the light when we are in the dark. Leonard Cohen sings, "***There is a crack in everything, that's how the light gets in.***" I see happiness that way. I see her paradox. I don't mind that she comes and goes and comes again. She's tenacious. She pushes through. She makes her way to us, sometimes when we least expect it. Often when we most need it.

So my darling, let it in, let it in, let it in. She won't stay long, but she will always come back.

Next year, on the anniversary of my mom's death, when I'm in tears and aching to talk to her, missing her voice, thinking about all the stories I want her to help me remember, John will find me somewhere in the house, maybe on the couch or maybe on my knees.

He will put his arms around me and ask,
  "Are you okay?"

And I will say,
  "No. But I will be."

Shawn Marie Turi
Business Strategist and Consultant
@shawnmarieturi

Chapter 9

This chapter is an honor to have in this book. Joe was an amazing person who dedicated his life to helping heal others. He was a distinguished figure in the field of psychotherapy, with over 25 years as a licensed trauma-informed psychotherapist. He was a ten-year military veteran, who also survived the Ukraine war. He was a devoted Father to six children and Grandfather to nine grandchildren. He sadly has passed away recently and will be remembered as brave, uplifting, wise, and extremely inspiring. Here is his chapter.

**"Rage Against the Dying of the Light:
Embracing Pain for a Life of Joy" by Joe Whitcomb**

In the grand human participation across our complex and collective collection of life experiences and existence, threads of pain and adversity are intricately woven alongside those of joy and peace, crafting a complex pattern that delineates our human experience. It is a natural inclination to flee from discomfort, yet there lies untapped wisdom and the potential for substantial growth within our struggles. The ethos of "Never Waste Your Pain" propels us to seek out significance and happiness in the throes of our most challenging periods. This narrative explores the journey of transforming our suffering into a vehicle for personal enhancement, resilience, and, ultimately, joy.

The Metamorphic Essence of Pain

Pain, be it of the soul or the flesh, frequently marks a watershed moment in our existence. It beckons for introspection, urging us to ponder deeply on our life's purpose, core values, and future direction. Far from being an experience to evade, embracing our pain can usher in a period of significant self-discovery and personal evolution. It is amidst these somber chapters that we uncover our true fortitude and resilience, learning to sail through life's tumults with dignity and steadfastness.

The Quest for Joy Amidst Adversity

The notion of finding joy in the face of adversity might seem counterintuitive, yet it is a possibility accessible to all. True joy is often not a byproduct of pain's absence but springs from the ability to unearth meaning and purpose regardless of it. To achieve this, several pathways can be explored:

- **Pursuit of Growth**: Every ordeal of pain should be viewed as an opportunity for self-improvement. Reflect on the lessons each experience imparts and how it can sculpt you into a more refined individual.

- **Cultivation of Gratitude**: By concentrating on the elements of your life worthy of thankfulness, gratitude redirects your attention from deficits to the abundance you possess, engendering a sense of fulfillment even amidst trials.

- **Forging Connections**: Open up about your struggles with those you trust. Such exchanges foster empathy and solidarity, reminding us of our collective journey through hardship.

- **Purposeful Pain**: Contemplate how your tribulations can serve others. Engaging in volunteer work, mentorship, or simply sharing your story can turn your pain into a beacon of hope and joy for both you and others.
- **Dedication to Self-Care**: Commit to activities that rejuvenate your spirit, mind, and body. Healing and rediscovering life's joys are contingent upon prioritizing self-care.

The Crucible of Resilience

Resilience stands as the conduit from suffering to joy. This quality does not merely represent the ability to rebound from adversity but encompasses learning from these experiences and pressing forward with an invigorated spirit. Cultivating resilience involves nurturing a positive mindset, emotional intelligence, and a network of support. It acknowledges that while pain is an inescapable element of life, it does not encapsulate our identity. Our reaction to pain and our capacity for overcoming it are what truly mold our essence.

Navigating the Path of Gratitude: Embracing Contentment and Empowerment

The journey of gratitude can be challenging, especially when the desire for more and the fear of losing what we already have persistently arise. This struggle is not unique to you alone, but one shared by many. It often leads us to compare ourselves to others, fostering despair, anxiety, and even depression.

Recognizing this ongoing challenge, cultivating a daily practice of gratitude becomes all the more crucial. But what does this practice entail, and how do we cultivate a grateful heart? Let us embark on a journey of 'out-side-the-box' thinking that begins within our own hearts.

First and foremost, practicing gratitude does not mean settling for the current state of things. It involves acknowledging and appreciating your life as it is, without cursing the challenges or temporary limitations you encounter. Imagine finding yourself stranded on an island, desperately in need of water, food, and shelter. Rather than resenting the rain or lamenting the elusive coconut high up in a tree, you resourcefully create a tool, bring down the tree, construct a shelter from it, consume the coconut for nourishment and hydration, and ingeniously repurpose its shell to collect rainwater, ensuring sustenance even on sunny days. Gratitude lies in embracing and being grateful for what you have, while simultaneously envisioning and creating what lies ahead. The human experience is one of constant movement and the pursuit of a better life.

Moreover, gratitude entails expressing gratitude for the opportunities and resources within your reach. This wisdom has been passed down through the ages as teachings from our wisest cultures. Embrace this wisdom and shift your focus away from what you lack. Instead, direct your attention towards the abundance and potential inherent in what you already possess, no matter how seemingly modest. By adopting this mindset of appreciation, you tap into the wellspring of creativity and manifest the life you desire.

Release the preoccupation with scarcity and inadequacy. Instead, choose to cultivate an abundant mindset by focusing on the possibilities that lie within what you have. Recognize that gratitude is not synonymous with settling, but rather a catalyst for growth and transformation. By practicing gratitude, you initiate a process of designing and shaping your life experience, empowered by the resources and opportunities available to you.

Embracing the Journey

To never waste one's pain is to recognize it as a fundamental and enriching component of life's odyssey, a wellspring of insight, growth, and transformation. In seeking joy within adversity, we transcend mere survival to flourish, emerging not only more robust and resilient but deeply connected to the core of our being.

This exploration serves as an affirmation that the ability to discover joy amidst hardship characterizes the depth of the human spirit. It encourages us to seek out the light, even in the darkest corners, promising that with courage and an open heart, we can unveil the splendor and abundance life offers. By embracing our pain, we unlock the portal to a life replete with profound significance, resilience, and, ultimately, boundless joy.

This tale is not just an exploration but a testament to my journey, marked by my heartaches and heartbreaks in life, love, and relationships, a decade of military discipline, and a harrowing year in Kyiv, Ukraine, from July 2021 to July 2022. Amidst escaping the war and experiencing moments of sheer terror, I've learned the essence of finding light in the darkest corners. These experiences have reinforced my belief that with courage and an open heart, we can uncover the beauty and richness life has to offer. By embracing our pain, we open doors to a life filled with deep meaning, resilience, and boundless joy.

In conclusion, the path of "Never Waste Your Pain" to gratitude involves transcending the perpetual longing for more and the fear of loss by recognizing and embracing the blessings in your life. It requires finding contentment with what you have and an awareness of the possibilities it holds. Embrace the tenets of gratitude passed down from ancient cultures— the powerful connection between gratitude, creation, and a meaningful existence. Shift your focus from what is absent to what is present and create anew. Design your life experience with gratitude as your guiding principle. So, let us raise a toast to the journey of gratitude and the profound empowerment it brings. Cheers to a life crafted in gratitude!

Joe Whitcomb, PsyDc, LMFT
CEO @ Relationship Society
BondFire Project
Trauma-informed Spatial Computing
XR Therapy from the Omnivores for the Metaverse

"Do not go gentle into that good night,
Old age should burn and rave at close of day;
Rage, rage against the dying of the light." Dylan Thomas

Chapter 10
Becoming Happy: A Journey Through
Service and Leadership

I am a policymaker in education, an advocate, a business owner, a mother, and a newlywed wife. As a single mom for 14 years, I overcame sibling abuse and the limiting beliefs of high school counselors who said I should be a secretary because I had uneducated parents. Despite this discouragement, I earned my degree and became President of the school board. My journey is a testament to tenacity, service, and leadership in achieving happiness.

"Hi. My name is Gloria Ramos." I learned how to introduce myself while waitressing for a group of Toastmasters at Coco's Restaurant when I was 16 years old. I'm in my 50s now and that skill was a game-changer. I said my name with intention, and I became the person I always dreamt of confident, well-spoken, intelligent, successful... you get me right? Up until those days of listening in on those Toastmasters meetings week after week and learning to introduce myself with intention, I felt invisible to the world. Nothing I said was heard, and maybe I didn't want to be heard. I had secrets, and those secrets scared me, so I acted out and rarely spoke of them. My life was an inconvenient truth; I did not want to admit to those secrets, and even if I did, NO one would want to hear them.

I had a really happy childhood until the age of three. I would see grandma daily; my mom was home or working with my grandma for her family-run business, so I was around two of the fiercest women known. They loved me and made sure I was safe as they gave me an awesome example of hard work and love. I had a daddy who provided for us, worked in grueling conditions, and came home to adore me. What was lurking just under the surface was that I had a mother who was running on empty most of the time and had to deal with my much older six siblings, who were a blended bunch from hers and my dad's previous marriages. Most of my siblings were either drug addicts, alcoholics, emotionally unstable, needy, or plain problematic. In addition, my dad was an immigrant, new to this country, language, and culture. During the 1970s, this was an extra level of hardship in any relationship. When you add my dad's general shortcomings into that, you can see where it could be a perfect storm for the littlest child to be unattended and, unfortunately, abused. I just happened to win the trifecta by being abused by two brothers. I was physically, psychologically, and sexually abused. Neither knew about the other. I physically survived by not speaking. I remember not speaking to anyone for a year. I struggled with expressing and showing emotion.

During those Toastmasters' weekly meetings, I learned their member values were integrity, respect, service, and excellence. I believed in all of those values too. Although the group was a bunch of older men, I really felt like I was part of their group. I learned through serving them the cream of broccoli soup and coffee with an occasional sandwich. The message I heard while taking orders and trying to earn a good tip was simple: LEADERSHIP. I wanted to be a leader!

As I navigated into early adulthood, I often felt adrift, the weight of my childhood trauma casting long shadows over my life. It wasn't until I embraced the values I learned from Toastmasters that I began to see a path to happiness. Integrity meant facing my past honestly, respecting myself enough to seek help, and pursuing excellence in my healing journey. But it was service and leadership that truly transformed me.

Service, I discovered, was not just about helping others but about finding purpose. I started small, helping loved ones, friends, and teachers. I also volunteered at a free clinic. Every act of kindness, every moment of giving, slowly chipped away at the wall I had built around my heart. I began to understand that my pain, my story, could serve a greater purpose. By helping those in need, I was healing myself. Each smile, each thank you, felt like a balm to my wounded soul.

Leadership, on the other hand, was about reclaiming my voice. It was about standing tall and saying, "I am here, and I matter." I became a teacher and showed my students how to be strong by standing up for them, listening to them, and respecting them. I took on higher roles at work and eventually became a school board member, an elected official making policies for public education and making difficult decisions where others might fold. The more I led, the more I healed. I learned that true leadership is rooted in empathy, in the ability to connect and inspire through authenticity.

Combining service and leadership allowed me to rewrite my narrative. No longer was I the silent, invisible girl. I was a woman of strength and purpose, guiding others towards their own paths of healing and happiness. This journey was not easy; it was marked by setbacks and moments of doubt. But each step forward, no matter how small, was a victory.
To anyone reading this, seeking their path to happiness, I offer these tips:

1. **Embrace Service**: Find ways to give back to your community. Service brings purpose and connection, which are essential for healing.

2. **Step into Leadership**: Don't be afraid to take charge of your life. Leadership builds confidence and resilience.

3. **Seek Support**: Healing is not a journey you have to take alone. Reach out for the help you need.

4. **Practice Self-Compassion**: Acknowledge your progress and forgive your setbacks.

5. **Set Boundaries**: Learn to say no and prioritize your well-being.

6. **Stay Persistent**: Keep moving forward, even when it's hard.

Becoming happy is not about erasing the past but about building a future where you can thrive. By embracing service and leadership, you can transform your pain into power and create a life filled with purpose and joy.

So, today Introduce yourself with intention. Say your name out loud and claim your space in the world. Serve others with an open heart and lead with empathy and strength. You'll likely find that happiness was always there, and you can find it over and over again.

Gloria Ramos
Life and Legacy Coach
www.gloriaramos.com

Chapter 11
Words To Live By

My name is Morris Hayes. I am a keyboardist, music producer, and songwriter. I had the amazing honor of playing keyboards for artists such as Maceo Parker (James Brown), Mazarati, The Time, and last but certainly not least, Prince. I also served as his music director as well for part of my tenure with the Purple icon. I was born in a small town in Arkansas called, Pine Bluff. My musical journey began in the 60's like a few I have come across in this industry, in the church. I was exposed to the likes of Mahalia Jackson, Aretha Franklin, and James Cleveland, among others, and I had an amazing keyboardist at my church who inspired me.

As I got older, I became an avid dancer and roller skater. I also started playing sports in school. These things became front and center with me along with playing the organ. I started to do well in those areas as I went on. I was granted a scholarship to the University of Arkansas at Pine Bluff for commercial art, but music quickly became my passion as I walked to my art classes passing by musicians practicing in these cubicles every day. I started to linger more and more until I could no longer resist the call of the music. I ended up getting involved with a campus band called, Polo, meeting guys who I would, to this day, still be friends with. This would be the spark that lit the fire for my music career. On December 17th,

1982, Prince came to my city of Pine Bluff for a concert. My whole band went to see him. While in the crowd watching the three acts, Vanity 6, The Time, and Prince, I was so enamored that I out loud declared that one day I would play with The Time, and as Prince came on I saw how amazing he was, I declared out loud again that I would also play with him. When I left that building, I knew that it was my destiny to be in the Minneapolis experience. I did not know how or when, but I knew somehow all roads lead to Minnesota.

Ten years later, I got my wish and was asked to join Prince's New Power Generation. As it was told to me by many around me of Prince's tough rehearsals and hard regiment, I quickly began to learn the hard way in which things could get to extraordinarily difficult levels in an instant. In many ways, it's what I had heard of what the military has with boot camp. The stress levels were incredibly high. So much so that when I would drive into the garage and see his car my stomach would get upset. I had to learn how to focus and figure out how not to be intimidated. I had to rely on every bit of advice I had garnered from my parents and my mentor, Craig Rice, so that I could function outside of fear and the overwhelming thoughts of my inferiority to the other players and Prince. Several times I thought of quitting due to the pressure, but the fear of failure was greater than the anxiety of all that training. After all, I didn't want to become the laughingstock of my peers but I felt I would let my whole town down. I felt I had the weight of the world on my shoulders.

I was very fortunate for my mom and dad, who taught me so many lessons that would become invaluable for me as I ventured into the rock and roll life. Sure, you hear about things that have happened to others and all the stories, but you never know until you cross that threshold. One of the absolute best things my mom did for me was giving me a book by the minister Charles Capps called, "The Tongue: A Creative Force". It would be one of the greatest tools in my toolbox, as it relates to how things came to be for me, as I see it, and how to deal with situations as they arrived. Reading this book, it taught me that what comes out of my mouth was paramount as it related to claiming things into existence and the importance of the words you use having power. Another great thing that I learned of was the so-called, 90/10 Principal. What the 90/10 Principal suggested is, with everything that happens to you, 10% is a cluster pop, and it is what it is. With the other 90%, how you react to the situation determines the outcome. To me, this was paramount as it taught me to think about my reaction to situations and its repercussions before I acted. I learned to lean on my family and friends when things got tough, and that support buoyed me. The main thing is I came to understand and to realize that my faith in God was what saved me more times than I can count. That was the balance. That was the thing when I felt I had no place to turn, I had refuge. My dear mother Maxine and Captain Moses "Rabbit' Hayes, by nurturing my faith, gave me the tools to make it in this life.

A couple of things that helped me that might help you: speak things into the universe verbally. An example is when I once was watching Soul Train in 1979 and saw a keyboardist and now friend, Patrice Rushen, performing. She was playing a keyboard called a Fender Rhodes. A friend of our family was staying at our home and was also watching as I declared I wanted one and she said she owned one and did not like it. She gave it to me. Had I not said it out loud, I would not have gotten it. Another key lesson, It isn't a mistake until you stop.

Morris Hayes - Keyboardist/Producer - Prince and The New Power Generation
www.morrishayes.com
Instagram: @hayes.morris
Facebook: https://www.facebook.com/morrishayesmusic
Facebook: https://www.facebook.com/MrMorrisKHayes
X: @MrMorrisHayes
LinkedIn: www.linkedin/in/morris-hayes-3
YouTube: @MorrisHayes
Photo credit for cover photo; Jan Van Heck

Chapter 12
Becoming the Happiest Person in the Room

Hello, I'm Maria Mizzi. I am a certified nutrition coach and an expert in Neuro-Linguistic Programming (NLP), specializing in weight loss and personal transformation. My journey has been one of profound self-discovery, overcoming personal struggles, and embracing a holistic approach to health and happiness. This chapter reflects my story, my struggles, and the insights I've gained along the way. It's designed to guide you toward a life filled with energy, confidence, and joy.

There was a time when walking into a room drained me of my energy and confidence. I felt like I left my true self at the door, overshadowed by insecurities and self-doubt. Anxiety often took over, leaving me powerless and overwhelmed by negative thoughts. I constantly searched for something to fill the void. At the time, food was a quick fix, leading to weight gain and even more diminished confidence. What I was truly hungry for was a deeper connection with myself.

Years of feeling trapped in this cycle pushed me to a breaking point. I decided that something had to change. I no longer wanted to be the person who felt small and insignificant. I yearned for transformation. So, I embarked on a journey of self-discovery, immersing myself in the study of psychology, spirituality, nutrition, and the human body.

The path was long and challenging, but eventually, I unearthed the shocking truth about diets and discovered the real path to lasting change. To create lasting change, I had to dismantle conventional dieting wisdom piece by piece. True transformation, I learned, is a lifestyle change that affects every level of your being. It's not something you try for a while and then abandon; it's a permanent shift in how you live your life.

One of the most significant discoveries I made was the cyclical nature of emotions and food. Negative emotions often lead to poor food choices, which in turn generate more negative emotions like guilt and shame. This vicious cycle traps us in a loop of sadness, anxiety, and unhealthy eating habits. I had to understand and break this cycle to find my path to happiness.

Through my research and personal experiences, I identified three primary emotions that often deter us from our path: boredom, anger, and anxiety. Boredom, for instance, often stems from a feeling of emptiness, leading to mindless eating while engaging in activities like scrolling through social media or dealing with accumulated disappointments. Recognizing this, I began to fill my time with meaningful activities that nourished my soul and kept my mind engaged.

Anger, a strong defensive emotion accompanied by a sense of revenge, is often linked to frustration over our inability to change a situation. I found that eating out of anger was a form of self-punishment that only led to more suffering. To counter this, I practiced forgiveness—both towards myself and others—and sought constructive ways to channel my frustration, such as through exercise or creative expression.

Anxiety, a mixture of fear and expectation that weakens and weighs us down, often drove me to seek comfort in food. This habit, I discovered, could be traced back to childhood. By acknowledging my anxiety and addressing its root causes, I was able to develop healthier coping mechanisms. Mindfulness and meditation became my tools for calming my mind and reducing my anxiety.

With these insights, I began to craft a vision for my life. I wanted to wake up in the morning feeling refreshed and energized, with a calm mind and a body radiating with energy, ready to embrace a life I loved. This vision became my guiding star, showing me that such a life was achievable.

Transformation requires change, and the first step is awareness. I had to become aware of my habits and how I might be sabotaging myself. Only then could I successfully transform my mind, body, and spirit. True nourishment, I discovered, comes from a place of connection, not resentment. I started by connecting with myself, both inside and out, beginning with gratitude. Every day, I reminded myself of the good things my body, mind, and spirit did for me. This connection guided me towards a healthier, happier life.

Throughout my journey, I developed several practical tips for transformation that I still use today:

- **Awareness**: Pay attention to your habits and emotions. Recognize the patterns that lead to poor food choices and negative feelings. Choose something you love about yourself, write it down, and read it throughout the day.
- **Gratitude**: Cultivate gratitude for your body, mind, and spirit. Appreciate the positive aspects of your life and let this gratitude fuel your transformation. Smile! Physically smiling can literally convince your brain to be in a better mood.
- **Connection**: Build a deeper connection with yourself. Understand your needs and desires, and nourish

yourself from a place of love and respect. Take a walk in nature. Nature connects us with our authentic selves. Listen to what nature is telling you and heed its advice.

- **Holistic Approach**: Focus on the body, mind, and spirit. True transformation involves nurturing all aspects of your being. Tune into the physical sensations of your emotions. Track your food and moods until you feel a new rise of energy and confidence.
- **Lifestyle Change**: Embrace transformation as a permanent lifestyle change, not a temporary fix. Commit to living a life that supports your health and happiness. Create a nourishing environment. Make choices that validate your self-worth and confidence, connect with yourself and others, and live in the bliss of your life daily.

By following these steps, I became the happiest person in the room, and you can too. Take the happiness quiz and find out how you're approaching happiness and ways to move closer to becoming the happiest person in the room.

Maria Mizzi

Visit www.MariaMizzi.com/happy

Chapter 13
Get Moving

Put all your unhappiness aside, life is beautiful, be happy.

I am Laurel Janssen Byrne, a writer, and native Southern Californian. Growing up with beautiful year-round weather, I have always enjoyed outdoor activities, like swimming, hiking, and running. As an avid exerciser, daily movement is an important part of my life. I sleep better, deal with stress better... I simply feel better overall. Daily movement is like breathing for me. After moving to New York for graduate school, I quickly discovered my love of walking. New York City is a wonderful walking town. Walking reminds me of my feisty, auburn-haired grandmother, Annie, who was an avid walker, and used movement as a conduit for her inspiring, long life.

Annie had just arrived in New York City in December 1928. 24 years young with only $10 in her pocket, she had unlimited excitement for her visit. Having grown up in rural Scotland and a recent immigrant to Canada, Annie found New York to be dazzling. December's icy grasp kissed her rosy cheeks. With limited funds for street cars and subway trains, Annie walked the length of Manhattan, moved by its pulse, discovering the city's unique nooks and interesting crannies. Corner shops *and sparkling streetlights thrilled her. With her twinkling green eyes wide open, the city's energy kept her moving, despite the cold and her growing hunger.*

*The warm, red lights of a small Chinese restaurant beckoned to her. Longevity Noodle House ... her first Chinese food...ever. White tablecloths draped cozy tables. A hurried waiter caught her eye peeping through the window, and in an instant, he swept her in through the swinging front door and seated her in the corner booth. Warm, pungent aromas wafted as she eyed from her table each passing person. First, a hot pot of tea arrived, followed by a plate of steaming vegetable noodles, placed quickly by the bustling waiter, his white cloth draping his arm. Then more tea, and finally, her bill and a cookie. $2 was the total, written in lovely script with a happy face jotted next to Thank You - Come Again Please! Annie had never had a fortune cookie. Looking inquisitively into her waiter's helpful face, he replied with a gesture for her to crack the cookie in two. "Your fortune, Miss," he whispered with a slight nod of his head. Noodles in her belly and tea in her cup, she broke open the cookie and read its optimistic message: **Put all your unhappiness aside, life is beautiful, be happy.** The waiter hadn't charged her for the tea. She smiled her thanks to him and ventured back to walk Manhattan's undiscovered avenues.*

Grandma Annie told me that story hundreds of times. I spent my childhood imagining her, moving through the city. She often took me out for Chinese food, retelling those memories. *"Why were you walking so much?"* I'd ask. *"Because I could. Movement, quite simply, makes me happy,"* she emphasized. Into her early 90s, she walked daily. I could hardly keep up with her as a child, my small, fatigued legs almost skipping to keep pace with her brisk, sturdy strength. And decades later, there I was, walking in the very same city. I could feel Annie's energy in my stride.

And still today, like her, daily movement quite simply makes me happy, the daily connecting of my body and my mind. Movement. I imagine my brain and body waking together, connecting like a cord plugging into a live socket, and energizing for another day of exercise, thinking, creating, loving, and doing. Movement has become a metaphor for progress in my life. On the best days, I feel strong and energized and healthy, clear of mind and purpose, prioritized goals met. And on the worst days, with aches or pains or losses or failures, I feel thankful to have a body to move, one foot in front of the other, sometimes slowly, but always surely, moving toward what's next.

I am often inspired by my neighbor while I'm out for my walks. He is paralyzed and moves only with a wheelchair. On his daily rides, I make certain to wave to him. He cannot wave back, but he sees me as our eyes meet. He is getting his movement, for his mind and soul. He is a great reminder to me that movement can be incorporated into our lives, you just have to get started.

Here's more inspiration:

<u>Move your body by starting slowly</u>

You never regret a workout, no matter how short or simple. Unpopular opinion, I love to exercise. When I move my body and my breath, I feel energized, calm, and in control of myself and my goals. I enjoy hiking, yoga, Pilates, strength training, and I love a good walk. Walks are great for your heart, brain, and lungs. Try a short walk in your neighborhood to begin or finish your day. Need a distraction? Focus on the architectural style of the homes in your neighborhood or the types of wildlife you encounter along the way. Listen to music, books or interesting podcasts during your journey. If you don't share my love of fitness, try a short stretch at home to get started.

Meet a friend

For many, having a friend or accountability partner motivates them to show up and stay consistent. I like to meet friends for walks, Pilate's classes and at the gym to strength train. We get to spend time together and catch up, all while doing something positive for our bodies and minds.

Move your breath

Movement also comes in the form of breath work and meditation. By moving your breath, you slow your racing thoughts, decrease your stress levels and calm your mind. As your breath moves in and out of your relaxing body, your heart rate slows, helping with anxiousness and fatigue. This can improve sleep (which is golden), your mental state, and your overall health.

Laurel Janssen Byrne
Writer
Find me on Instagram: @miss_laurel_

Chapter 14
The Beauty in Hope

Even as a young child, I have always believed in miracles. I have always had big dreams. Dreams so big that people told me there's no chance that they would happen, but I always had hope. One of my biggest passions as an energy healer, Akashic Records practitioner and astrologer is to help people to heal and let go of what is blocking them stepping into their authentic selves, and to inspire them to live the life of their wildest dreams.

I believe that manifesting and living your most joyful, most authentic life is all about having hope. Finding the glimmers of hope inside of you even when you can't see it, and holding onto that hope when the world tells you otherwise. Believing that everything is going to work out, even when we don't have tangible proof. There are endless possibilities, and miraculous things that can happen at any moment. You just have to find the hope to keep going.

Dear Future Self,

I'm sorry that I doubted you and your capacity to manifest exactly what you knew was meant for you. I'm sorry for the times that I lost hope. The times when I didn't have faith in myself and what my heart knew was coming. There were times when my dreams felt so big and so out of reach that I doubted they could come true, but you knew all along. They say that there are future versions of ourselves that already have the things we want to manifest. I believe the reason I wanted these things so deeply in my heart and never gave up despite all of the challenges was because my soul knew that the future was already there. I was born with big dreams, a very strong intuition, endless optimism, and the tenacity to keep going when things get tough. I am not someone who gives up on my dreams. I believe my soul knew all along that I would live a life of my wildest dreams. I have healed, and I have outgrown so many versions of myself to get here. I'm so proud of the work I've done to become the most authentic version of myself. I've unwrapped the layers of conditioning and released who the world taught me I "should" be to reveal who I was born to be, who I really am inside. I will continue to do this work, and I will try to remember how far I've come the next time I doubt myself. I will give myself the grace of knowing that I am a soul living a human experience, and this is all part of my soul's growth. It's all part of the classroom that my soul chose in this lifetime. I will have gratitude for each version of myself that never gave up. I will do my best to honor and celebrate every step of my journey in this beautiful life, and I will continue to help others to do the same.

Lots of Love,
Stefanie

There have been times in my life when I didn't know how I was going to go on. One of those times was when my mom passed away. I was twenty-five years old, and she was my best friend and my rock. It was sudden and unexpected, and it destroyed my whole world as I knew it. I remember lying in bed in the weeks after, not knowing how I could go on and live life without her. It was a very dark time, and thankfully I found small glimmers of hope that kept me going. Now I have a ten-year-old daughter who is the love of my life, and we have the most beautiful relationship, just like my mom and I had. I get to honor my mom every day by giving Chloe the unconditional love that my mom always gave me.

When I'm in a place where I'm having trouble accessing hope, I take a mental inventory of times when everything has worked out in my life. Most of the time it has worked out better than I ever could have imagined. That doesn't mean I haven't struggled to get there. I have a big soul, and I've had a lot of big lessons. Challenges are part of the journey, but when I look back I don't focus on the challenges. I focus on the person I've become through these experiences. Let your mind recall a time when everything worked out for you. A time when you thought to yourself, "Wow, I did it! I made it!" Feel that energy of joy and relief within you now.

Let's do an exercise together. You can come back to this exercise whenever you want to. Close your eyes and see yourself on a path walking through the woods in a beautiful place. You're walking slowly down this path, listening to the birds chirping and feeling the sunlight through the trees. With each step you're shedding what no longer serves you. The baggage that you've been holding onto, that is weighing you down and keeping you stuck, is falling off with every step like a heavy backpack. You feel lighter and lighter as you go. You see a clearing ahead with the most vibrant sunshine.

Before you reach the end of the path you look back and see the past versions of yourself watching you. You look back at these versions of yourself with gratitude, love, and pride in how far you've come and how much you've healed and transformed. You can see now that each version was exactly what you needed to get to where you are today. You smile at each version of yourself, knowing that you wouldn't be who you are today without them. Before you reach the end of the path take a moment to envision your dream life. Not the life you think you should have, but the life that you've always dreamed of. Your most joyful, authentic life where you shine so bright with your unique soul radiance. What does that life look like? Once you have that vision, feel the warmth of the sun on your face as you step into your new timeline, giving yourself a fresh start today.

Stefanie Greer
Energy Healer/Meditation Facilitator/Speaker/Coach
www.sgenergyhealing.com

Chapter 15
The Dao

My name is Somer Reign. Two years ago, my life turned upside down, and I lost my grandma, my animals, my place to live, and my daughter walked out of my life.

I had been living with my grandma taking care of her for 17 years while raising my daughter, and I had told my grandmother I would be there until the end. My daughter Mersadiez lived with us for 10 years, and then she met her Dad a year later. We decided that she was going to go live with him and get to know him better.

Mersadiez spent many years going back an -forth to both houses, then after Grandma passed away, she stopped coming home because said it "felt weird." After a few weeks passed, she chose not to talk to me and blocked me from all internet and phone. I don't know why she chose this. It has been very troubling. Over the years, I've had to wipe the tears away and just let go and let God.

I needed more than angels to help me through this devastating time in my life, I needed a community and tools to help me stay focused and keep my mindset strong as I navigated into another state with only a few sentimental things and a van to live in.

That's when I started the Dao zoom community with a friend in Canada named Matthew. Together with a few friends we learned these ancient Dao principles that changed my life. We created a Dao book and share the book with friends who are looking for a change in their life and now study from the principles every day.

I have learned over the years how to shift my mind and not have fearful thoughts that stopped me in my tracks before. I learned how to ask for help and not do everything on my own. I also learned how to be calm, patient and compassionate in every rocky situation I've been in over the years.

Here is what helped me the most.

The Cup and the Shadow

In the intricate landscape of our minds, there exists a powerful light at the core of our being; a beacon that illuminates our thoughts and manifests our reality. This guiding principle is essential, especially when we find ourselves hindered by self-imposed barriers. Consider the experience of repeatedly trying and failing at new diets: the initial excitement of weight loss followed by discouragement and eventual regression. This cycle reflects a deeper need to reshape our internal patterns and mindset to achieve lasting change.

Have you ever tried a new diet? You keep trying different diets. You get excited and you lose weight. Later, if the number on the scale doesn't go down you get discouraged. You quit and gain the weight back. You try it again, and the cycle continues. This is the pattern. To get results, you have to go within and create new patterns in your mind, body, and soul.

Our thoughts are the content of the cup. It's like trying to change the shadow (the external), by doing what's outside of you to move the cup. Instead, you have to change your mind first. It doesn't work to change the external world experience instead of changing the internal world. Why don't these diets work? You're always trying to change the shadow, which is your pattern.

When you get up above the clouds, it's always sunny. There are no clouds. This is like moving the cup. When you change your mindset and inner world, you are in the present moment and there is no suffering It's always a sunny day.

Another way to understand this would be that the third dimension is the material world and our five senses. The fourth dimension is your mind, your ego, and your belief system. The fifth dimension is your karma, angels, God, and your higher self.

So imagine this cup is on a table. If I move the cup, the shadow goes with it because it is third dimension. The cup is the fourth dimension, which means at our third-dimension reality, health bank account, and relationships are determined by your fourth-dimensional reality, which is your thinking, so if you don't change your thinking, you cannot change your life. It's like trying to move the shadow of a cup without moving the cup. Sometimes I've changed my thinking and that still doesn't work. I still don't change my life, so then you go to a fifth dimension.

Sometimes it doesn't feel motivating to try to change your life. You think that will never happen or I've got the rest of my life to figure that out. These are excuses, which is the roommate in our head, or our ego, which convinces us to not move the cup. Most of the time if we feel in pain or we are suffering, we just try to move the shadow, which is suffering.

It is like trying to cut out blackberry bushes from your backyard by cutting the stem of the blackberry to get rid of the thorns. You think I will go relax now and not deal with my life, and then the blackberry bush grows back. We all know if you clip that bush, it just keeps coming right back.

I'm in pain again. Why does this happen? You want to give up and think this is just my life. You give more excuses and convince yourself that it's just the way it is. We need to pull out the roots of the negative seed, inside of our consciousness, so the blackberry Bush, the suffering, does not come back. If you spend your life just barely putting in the effort to move the shadow, life's not worth it, then the blackberry bush will scratch you forever.

True transformation requires us to delve beyond superficial changes and address the root causes within our consciousness. Just as cutting the stem of a blackberry bush will only provide temporary relief from its thorns, so too will minimal efforts to change our external circumstances prove insufficient. By uprooting the negative seeds within and shifting our mindset, we can transcend the repetitive patterns of suffering and cultivate a life of lasting fulfillment and growth.

email me for the free book," How to Dao Wisdom for The Now".

Somer Reign
Spiritual Leader, Author
Somerreign3@gmail.com

Chapter 16
Complete Self-Acceptance

I am Melissa Tori, a wife, dog mom, proud aunt, #1 best-selling author, and certified Life Wellness Coach. My passion is helping midlife women fall back in love with themselves and their lives. After losing 130 pounds naturally and overcoming personal challenges, I discovered that true healing begins with complete self-acceptance. This practice has been transformative for me and many others, leading to happiness, healing, and inner peace.

From an early age, due to family circumstances, I often felt alone. Food became my comfort, leading to a cycle of loneliness, ridicule, and self-loathing. Throughout my teen years, I battled an eating disorder and looked for validation through unhealthy relationships. In adulthood, the pattern continued in my career, seeking unhealthy validation in climbing the corporate ladder.

At 32, my life hit rock bottom after failed fertility attempts and a painful divorce amidst a toxic work environment. In severe depression, I turned to food for comfort, leading to more isolation. I felt worthless and unlovable. I genuinely believed if I died, no one would care. One lonely night, I dared to ask myself why these patterns persisted and painfully realized I was the common thread. I sought help, seeing the need for personal accountability.

Complete self-acceptance is more than just acknowledging our flaws; it is about leaning into them with compassion and embracing our entire being with love. Accepting ourselves with grace is essential for true healing.

We can transform bitterness through understanding and awareness. Recognizing our worth and leaning into faith can facilitate this transformation. I lean into my faith and the belief that I am supported by the Universe and God. When faced with a situation, I ask myself if I can control it. If the answer is no, I make a conscious decision to let it go. Shifting my focus to something that brings me joy helps me maintain a positive outlook. This practice has been instrumental, helping me let go of bitterness and curate a more understanding mindset.

Recognizing and accepting our role in recurring situations is key to breaking negative cycles. Personal accountability brings about growth. I guide people through situation analysis, helping them see common threads and personal involvement. Often, simply being heard helps them realize their role in these patterns. When low or critical thoughts come in, I remind myself of my achievements and focus on things that bring positivity. I share stories of my struggles with clients to show them they are not alone, and that real change is not only possible but also achievable.

Reflect on daily experiences, identify negative thoughts, and replace them with positive ones to reframe and rewire our brains for a brighter outlook. One effective practice is gratitude journaling. Write down three things you are grateful for each day and reflect on their positive impact. This simple exercise shifts your focus from what is wrong to what is right, nurturing a more positive outlook. Once we are in a better frame of mind, we can more easily accept our role in situations and take steps toward personal growth. True healing involves embracing all parts of ourselves—physical, emotional, and spiritual.

Inner child work is another powerful practice in the journey toward self-acceptance. In your journal, engage in conversations with your younger self. Assure them that you, as the adult, are providing the necessary love and care. This helps heal past wounds and fosters self-compassion. For instance, write affirmations to your younger self, such as, "I am here for you, and I love you just as you are." This practice helps integrate all parts of you, leading to a more harmonious and accepting self-view.

Incorporating fitness and exercise into your daily routine is vital for promoting well-being and self-acceptance. Aim for at least 20 minutes of movement each day, whether walking, yoga, or any physical activity you enjoy. This supports physical and mental health. Focus on letting go of negative thoughts and emotions through guided meditations, fostering relaxation and inner peace. Additionally, sleeping meditations can improve rest and overall well-being, helping you process emotions and maintain a calm state of mind.

Complete self-acceptance is a transformative practice that unlocks the door to your true self. It allows you to love and accept yourself wholly, leading to inner peace and happiness. In utilizing these principles and practices, you can begin a journey of profound personal growth and healing. Start with simple practices like gratitude journaling, daily reflections, and inner child affirmations. Integrate physical activities and meditation into your routine to support holistic healing. As you continue to practice self-acceptance, you will notice a significant shift in your outlook and overall well-being.

Taking personal accountability for your role in life's challenges can be daunting, but it is crucial for breaking negative cycles and fostering growth. Remember, the journey of self-acceptance is ongoing. It requires patience, compassion, and a commitment to consistently practice these principles. Create a support system with people who understand and respect your journey. If a solid support system seems unreachable, seek out support groups, a Life Coach, or educational materials to help you along the way.

I encourage you to take a chance on yourself, believe in your worth, and start your journey toward self-acceptance today. Begin with these simple practices and watch as they transform your life. By embracing self-acceptance, you open the door to a life filled with happiness, healing, and inner peace. You deserve to love and accept yourself fully, and with dedication and practice, you can achieve this transformation. Take the first step today on your journey to a more fulfilling and self-loving life.

We all have the potential for profound self-acceptance and growth. If I can, you can. I believe in you.

Melissa Tori

Life Wellness Coach

www.melissatori.com

Chapter 17
The Healing Power of Creativity
Discover the Artist Within You

Hello! I'm Claudia Guardado, an artist, entrepreneur, and passionate advocate for the transformative power of creativity. Welcome to my story—a journey through the ups and downs of life, and how rediscovering my creative spark brought healing and joy back into my world. Whether you're a seasoned artist or someone who hasn't picked up a paintbrush since grade school, I hope my story inspires you to reconnect with your own creative spirit.

The Early Days: Discovering My Creative Spark

From the age of eight, painting became my sanctuary. My first encounter with a brush and canvas opened a world where colors danced, and imagination soared. Encouraged by my parents, I enrolled in art classes, eagerly absorbing every lesson. My instructor, recognizing my innate talent, eventually told my parents there was nothing more she could teach me. At first, this news saddened me, leaving a void where my art classes once were. However, the joy of creating art never left me; it lingered like a comforting presence, always ready to return when needed.

School projects became my outlet for creativity, each one a new adventure. The thrill of assignments that allowed me to paint or craft fueled my enthusiasm. This passion stayed with me through the years, a quiet but constant companion. Yet, as life moved forward, my artistic pursuits took a backseat to other responsibilities and expectations.

The Dormant Years: Creativity on Hold

Life has a way of leading us down unexpected paths. I got married and spent 22 years in a relationship where, ironically, the very qualities my husband admired in me—my creativity and love for painting and singing were stifled. During this period, my artistic endeavors faded into the background. My time and energy were consumed by the roles of wife and caregiver, especially during my father's final years. Losing him was a profound experience, but it also reconnected me with a fundamental part of myself.

My father had always been a beacon of support and inspiration. His passing reminded me of the joy and healing that creativity brought into my life. It was during these challenging years that I realized how much I had suppressed a vital part of who I was. Art and music, my lifelong companions, had been neglected, and with them, a significant source of my happiness.

Rediscovery and Rebirth

The end of my marriage in 2018 marked the beginning of a new chapter. Amidst the emotional turmoil, I found solace in rediscovering my artistic passions. painting, singing, and crafting became therapeutic outlets, helping me navigate the waves of change. In 2015, even before my divorce, a fortuitous partnership led to the creation of a music production company. This venture rekindled my creative spirit and provided a glimpse of the joy that could still be mine.

In August 2019, I took another bold step by launching my own sock company. This endeavor was not just a business; it was a symbol of my resilience and creativity. The success was swift, with the return on investment realized within the first three months. I felt invincible, riding a wave of renewed purpose and passion.

The Pandemic: A Test of Resilience

Then, in March 2020, the world changed. The pandemic brought life to a standstill, and with it, my flourishing businesses faced unprecedented challenges. Isolation and uncertainty loomed large, and once again, I found myself in a state of despair. The sock company and the music production business both struggled to survive in the new reality. Depression set in, and for a time, it felt as if the joy and creativity that had once lifted me were slipping away.

It was during this dark period that a call from a friend reignited my creative flame. She invited me to host a paint night for her vaccinated family, a simple request that had profound consequences. The evening was a success, reminding me of the power of art to bring people together and uplift spirits.

Create With Me: A New Beginning

Inspired by that one paint night, I began offering virtual art sessions. The response was overwhelming. People, starved for connection and creative expression, eagerly joined these sessions. What started as a few online gatherings quickly grew into a thriving business. I created a website, social media pages, and soon, "Create with Me" was born.

Through "Create with Me," I have had the privilege of helping others discover their own creative potential. From corporate events to intimate family gatherings, each session is a celebration of imagination and self-expression. Watching people light up as they paint, craft, and create has been one of the most rewarding experiences of my life.

Top Tips to Rediscover Your Creative Fire

1. **Start Small**: Don't overwhelm yourself with grand projects. Begin with small, manageable tasks like doodling or coloring. Let your creativity grow naturally.
2. **Set Aside Time**: Dedicate a specific time each day or week to your creative activities. Treat it like an important appointment you can't miss.
3. **Create a Space**: Find a quiet, comfortable place where you can focus on your art. Whether it's a corner of your room or a spot in the garden, make it your creative sanctuary.
4. **Embrace Imperfection**: Let go of the need for perfection. Creativity is about expression, not flawlessness. Enjoy the process without worrying about the outcome.
5. **Seek Inspiration**: Surround yourself with things that inspire you. Visit galleries, read books, listen to music, or explore nature. Inspiration can come from the most unexpected places.
6. **Connect with Others**: Join art groups, take classes, or participate in online forums. Sharing your work and experiences with others can be incredibly motivating.
7. **Keep Experimenting**: Try different mediums and techniques. Experimentation can spark new ideas and open up new avenues of creativity.

The Transformative Power of Creativity

Looking back, I realize that creativity has always been a lifeline for me. It provided an escape during childhood, a sense of identity in my youth, and a path to healing in adulthood. Rediscovering my creative passions has been a journey of self-rediscovery and empowerment.

Art and creativity have the power to heal, transform, and uplift. They connect us to our innermost selves and to each other. Through "Create with Me," I have witnessed firsthand the joy and fulfillment that creative expression can bring. It has taught me that no matter how lost we may feel, creativity can guide us back to ourselves.

As you explore the ways to heal your mind, body, and soul, I encourage you to embrace your own creativity. Whether it's painting, singing, writing, or any other form of artistic expression, allow yourself to be transported to another world. Let your imagination soar and your spirit be free. Creativity is not just a pastime; it is a powerful tool for healing and happiness. If my journey resonates with you, I invite you to connect with me. . Let's explore the transformative power of creativity together.

Claudia Guardado

www.createwithme.la

email; createwithme@gmail.com

Instagram @create.with.me.la

Chapter18
The Whisper Within

My name is Yesenia Garcia. I'm a real estate agent and mother of three wonderful boys. But beyond these roles, I am on an extraordinary journey, one that has transformed my life in ways I never imagined. I invite you to join me as I unfold the story of how my life was turned upside down and how, through embracing the unknown, I found a deeper connection to my true self and the divine.

In 2020, a series of events pushed me onto a path of spiritual seeking—a journey often referred to as a "Spiritual Crisis." I had just remarried, and "The Whisper Within," that persistent, mystical voice deep within, had been speaking to me for years. I was trying my best to live a "normal" life, and diving deep into spirituality didn't fit that life. The more I buried myself in routine, the louder the whisper grew, shaking my entire life's foundation.

In 2021, I was diagnosed with breast cancer. It didn't just halt the show; it stopped life as I knew it. When I received the news, it felt like a huge ocean wave came out of nowhere, smashing me against the rocks and drowning me in fear. The treatment plans the oncologists and surgeons proposed wasn't an option for me. "The Whisper Within" took the driver's seat, guiding me toward holistic healing and alternative therapies. Ignoring "The Whisper Within" was no longer an option. Trust me, I tried. But the more I tried to hold on, the worse it got. I reached the point where I couldn't keep up with life anymore. I literally felt like I was dying.

This path was the hardest I've walked in my life. Everything in my life crumbled to ashes. The life I had vanished. My marriage, my house, my business—all gone. The Yesenia I knew disappeared. I didn't recognize myself physically, emotionally, or mentally. "The Whisper Within" was loud and clear: "Let it fall apart, let go." Every time I thought I had hit bottom, there was more depth to explore. Depression, bitterness, and resentment weighed heavily on me. The things I thought defined who I was no longer existed. I trusted the Yesenia I used to be. She could get me through anything. Where is she? I had lost myself, and I was devastated.

Looking back now, I can see clearly that it wasn't until I had completely lost myself; my identity, and who I thought I was, that I could start calling my energy back to myself. I had hit rock bottom in every possible way. This process gave me an opportunity to free myself from my personal history. If I didn't have a personal history, I didn't have to live up to it. I didn't want to carry those heavy bags anymore. With nothing else left, all I had that gave me a sense of peace was prayer and meditation, which I held on to as if my life depended on it—because it did.

Solitude and embracing silence during this time was the greatest gift I gave myself. Meditation took me to that place within where I made conscious contact with Source/GOD. I realized that if I could get back to my Source, back to that feeling of being with spirit, that's where my true healing would take place.

In that moment, I understood this was so much bigger than healing cancer. Cancer had shown up to heal my life—mind, body, and spirit. I had been so resentful towards the idea of "everything happens for a reason" because I had no clue what the reason was. So, I made a conscious decision: if it's important for me to understand why I had to go through all those experiences, I'm done waiting for the reason to be revealed to me. I will assign meaning to it. I will decide for myself what it means. This new mindset empowered me.

So many unique gifts unfolded from what I thought was the worst time of my life. I've experienced pure magic, bliss, and joy—from mystical moments, to manifesting solutions to big financial issues, to helping others open their hearts and heal themselves. I've been on epic adventures to Costa Rica, the Amazon in Peru, and Mount Shasta, connecting with Mother Gaia. I visited small villages where I learned about nutrition, plant medicine, herbs, holistic healing, and breath work. I attended Dr. Joe Dispenza's events in beautiful locations like the Riviera Maya and Marco Island, making meaningful connections with like-minded souls. The greatest gift of life unfolded from all this travel: my heart opened, and I experienced unconditional love.

I am a powerful alchemist and healer. We all are. I never lost myself; on the contrary, I found who I AM. I am still integrating. It hasn't been easy, but I am grateful for every moment. Dr. Joe Dispenza teaches: "When you can look back and be truly grateful for every moment in your past, that's when you know true healing is happening." There is a new level of awareness, wisdom, and knowing, a different way of living my life. It has changed how I see and handle things, but more than anything, it has changed how I feel. I trust life. I still don't understand many things, but I do know what true love feels like, and I follow that every day.

When I was diagnosed with breast cancer, one of my biggest fears was the idea of "dying with my music still in me." Dr. Wayne Dyer wrote, "All of you have some music playing. We all show up here with a purpose. Don't die with your music still in you." I was not playing my music. It wasn't clear to me what my music was. Writing and talking about my journey has set me free. I Now Know What My Music Is—It's Playing Right Now. Are you listening to "The Whisper Within" you? What is your music? Are you playing it?

Yesenia Garcia

Real Estate Professional

YeseniaGarcia.RodeoRE.com

Chapter 19
Mindset

I'm Yvonne, a certified Life Coach specializing in mindset. I spent many years studying personal & professional development and the dynamics of having a healthy & loving relationship. My own healing journey meant overcoming divorce, grief from loss, and healing from some very difficult relationships. I hope to impact and inspire others to live their best life with the wisdom gained from life experiences and life lessons.

Mindset Healing

When I went through a divorce, I had been married for 30 years. Being married was all I knew, and pretty much my entire adult life thus far. I had to completely reinvent myself. I had to create my own stability and had no idea where or how to begin. I learned that a positive mind was key for me if I wanted to create a happy and peaceful life for myself.

We all go through challenges in life and everyone has his or her unique journey. We spend a lifetime learning how to do better and be better versions of ourselves so we can live a good life. When we learn from each other we can have that breakthrough. It gives us a new way to look at things – a fresh perspective and healing takes place. We feel lighter, brighter, and lifted while the only thing that changed is our mindset. If we can help our mindset in the first place, we can more easily let go of what is out of our control. Having our minds in a place that is centered and grounded is the first step to handling challenges with poise and grace. But how do we get there in a world that is fast-paced and demands for our time and attention are ever-increasing?

The first thing that you must do is take care of your health. Where do you begin you may wonder? Sleep as much as your body requires. This is usually between six and eight hours, so strive for eight. Let everything else go until you've had enough sleep. Your whole outlook on your life will change for the better when you are rested. You will face challenges with solutions you never thought of before with your new perspective. Not only that, but your whole body will function better.

The very next thing to address is nourishment. Make healthy choices when you can when it comes to what you put in your body. This is so important for how well you can focus on the things that really matter. Make sure you are hydrated and eating balanced meals. When you are putting good things into your body, your body is getting what it needs.

We all need endorphins, and you can get them in whichever way you choose. If you don't know where to begin, just go for a five-minute walk. Add a minute every day for a week, and you will be up to one mile in no time. Once you incorporate this habit, you will look forward to it and never not want to do it. At whatever level you begin, always listen to your body. You will see things differently and have a more positive outlook.

Have a "stress toolbox". Make a list of treats to keep handy, and also add things that feel good to you. Mine includes music, going for a walk, fresh flowers and scented candles. Pausing is also absolutely one of the best tools you can incorporate into your toolbox. When feeling overwhelmed or bombarded with tasks or communication, give yourself a moment to pause. Do not respond immediately in communication because you will most likely respond defensively. Pause, take some deep breaths, and take time to plan your next action, whether it's communication, making a to-do list, etc. Along with this, make a list of things that make you feel empowered and refer to it often. This will help to give you positive energy.

Be thankful in everything. Everything you go through is a steppingstone to the next part of your journey. Look for ways to grow from the experience. Take time to pause and reflect. Don't be hard on yourself. When we know better, we do better. Make a list of things you are thankful for and add to it every day. Think of the little things (like clean laundry), and then the big things (like a roof over your head). Whatever you focus on grows, so keep your focus on the good things you have, and you will attract more good things in your life.

Keep the words you speak positive. Our words are more powerful than we even realize. You will progress faster from any healing journey you are on by keeping the words you speak positive. Who do you admire? Think of celebrities, public figures, mentors, etc. How would they have handled a challenging situation like yours? If they truly are admirable, it would have been with poise, discretion, and by being the bigger person. Be that, always!

When you find yourself in a very deep period of change due to something traumatic in your life such as loss or divorce you will have time alone which can be extremely difficult. Don't fall into self-destructive habits, but instead, use the time to focus on yourself. Nurture yourself and seek self-growth. Find ways to become the best version of yourself. Don't be afraid of solitude, rather learn to embrace it.

Learn to surrender and let go. This may take some practice. Don't hold onto any resentment or vengefulness. Think about what is in your control. It is just yourself and your environment. Take care of those things and let the rest go. You can't control anyone else or how you are treated, but you can control how you respond and how you treat others. Always pause, then act with integrity, and most of all find your peace.

Healing from anything is a process, and I hope your journey is your road to peace.
Yvonne Lujan
www.yvonnelifecoach.com and yvonneclujan@gmail.com

Chapter 20
Cultivating Self -Love Daily

Hi, I'm Lilly Melgar. I've been fortunate enough to have enjoyed a long career as an Emmy nominated actress, an Emmy-winning producer, a director, and a TV host. Yet my most important and fulfilling role has been that of being a mother to the most extraordinary soul. And the thing that has impacted me the most has been my personal journey of spiritual growth toward realizing my authentic self.

There's a lot of talk about self-love. Most of us don't even know what that means and therefore struggle to access that often hidden part of ourselves. Through my journey, I've discovered that cultivating the love of self is a deeply personal, intuitive, and sacred process. It requires time, patience, and consistent self-care.

Reflecting on my path, I now understand that my self-love journey was fueled by profound pain and unexpected, crushing loss. In 2019, I endured a tumultuous divorce that left me emotionally bankrupt. That was only the beginning of a yearlong sojourn in grief. Nine months later, just as I was beginning to heal, my ex-husband tragically took his own life. The following day, the world locked down in response to Covid-19 as our family grieved and desperately tried to recover from the tragic loss. Then my father was diagnosed with leukemia, and witnessing his rapid decline shattered me. Within five and a half months, our family stood by his bedside as he peacefully transitioned, leaving us with a soul-crushing void that felt impossible to fill. Soon after, I said goodbye to my loyal protector, my beautiful dog Kane, leaving me feeling as if yet another part of my Spirit had been torn away. Each loss felt like a cruel blow, draining the very essence of life from my being. Lost and utterly broken, I became consumed by an unfamiliar darkness. Yet in that darkness, I discovered my capacity not only to endure but also to evolve from adversity. I was already vaguely aware of my resilience from a previous life-altering tragedy, but there were lessons waiting.

For me, that lesson involved courageously facing myself: the parts of me that felt unworthy, inadequate, and undeserving. I had to shed the facade in order to confront my pain, acknowledge my deepest fears, and wholeheartedly accept all the abandoned places within.

I lacked the bandwidth to continue any pretense or self-deception. For a bit, the shadows lurked, and I couldn't see my way out. I had heard this countless times, but nothing could be truer: "The only way out was 'through'." I had no choice but to reluctantly sit with the pain. I embraced the overwhelming regret, shame, and all other uninvited feelings that shed a harsh light on where I most needed healing. It was a brutal process of forgiveness, release, and self-discovery.

As I reflected, I realized all o which I had betrayed myself. All that I had passively allowed, weakly excused, and silently settled for. All the regrettable choices I had mindlessly made, and all the times I had simply "checked out". For the first time in my life, I could see all o which I had not loved myself. As painful as it was, I was no longer willing to look away. I felt it ALL. By confronting my darkness, I awakened to my authentic self. No more hiding, only a raw, unapologetic embrace of my true self. I had zero desire left to be anything other than me.

Beyond confronting inner demons, it was time to embrace my inner child. The one I neglected every time I chose anything other than love. It was time to reconnect to my true essence, the place within me where innocence still reigned.

I began with gratitude, feeling my way into all that was "right" in my world, despite the overwhelming sense of what was wrong. I was focusing on the blessings and not the losses. I began recognizing and affirming all of the good that was already present, and the veil of grief lost its grip on how I was witnessing my life, allowing me to see with a renewed perspective.

If this resonates with you at all, then I'd love to share a couple of the ways in which I cultivate self-love.

1. GRATITUDE - Life is unpredictable. No one is immune from the unexpected. Gratitude isn't some magic word. "It's a conscious choice to become present, aware, and thankful for all that *is* right and all that *is* in your favor." Incorporating gratitude into your daily life is the tool that holds the superpower to completely shift your life experience.

My personal gratitude practice consists of beginning my day by acknowledging things I'm genuinely grateful for. I write in my gratitude journal and sometimes simply feel my way into how grateful I am to wake up in my cozy bed with my perfectly sweetened organic coffee in my favorite mug and the calming silence of the morning, allowing me to tune inward - the warmth of gratitude beginning to expand my heart. By expressing gratitude for your current blessings, you open yourself up to experience even greater abundance. As I end my day, I again write what I am thankful for. I reflect and celebrate all that went well. This practice not only uplifts my thoughts before falling asleep but also rewires my brain to focus on what is right in my world.

YOUR TRIBE - Gratitude and choosing my beliefs wisely completely transformed my perception. I found myself not only attracting but feeling attracted to different types of people. I became surrounded by the most empowering, uplifting, and inspiring souls! I cannot communicate enough the tremendous impact this has had on my life. Not only does life get richer, but it calls you to higher ground. Choosing people in your life you can trust, who are not only supportive but genuinely rooting for you, and with whom your values align sets you up for success. These are the people who will remind you of all that is right with you when you inevitably forget: the ones who will guide you back to awareness when you temporarily lose sight, the ones who will celebrate you when you win, and the ones who will hold your hand when you don't. Your chosen family IS your greatest investment in life. They are your fuel, your mirror, and your team. These are the people who bring out your best and inspire you to be better. These are the ones who care enough to speak the truth in love when needed. Simply put, the ones who will carry you through. Save yourself unnecessary drama, as life is tough enough by nature, and make sure you choose people you admire and respect, as they will upgrade the quality of your life exponentially. "If you want to go fast, go alone; If you want to go far, go together."

Lilly Melgar
Actress/Director/Producer
@lillymelgarofficial

Chapter 21
Overcoming Imposter Syndrome

I am Cassandra Wilson, an avid tennis fan, music lover, and travel enthusiast. I am also an experienced coach, facilitator, and consultant with over 15 years of developing leaders to reach their fullest potential. I focus on practical application, deep listening, and intuition with clients to increase their awareness to become trustworthy, productive leaders.

It's a term I'd heard for years – imposter syndrome. At the time, I believed it to be something that happened to "other" people, those who hadn't accomplished much or who were trying to "fit in" to places they didn't belong. I remember feeling pity for them because that could never happen to me. I mean, I worked my ass off for everything, I earned every promotion I did (and didn't) receive. I'm the *realest* person out there! True to myself, strong, and resilient; until it happened to me.

I was in between jobs and looking for work. I worked with a brilliant woman who helped me write a great resume that got me noticed quickly. She had me focus on my strengths, *Clifton Strengths*, specifically. I landed multiple interviews with companies and their executives. I accepted an offer I would later find was tailor made for me. Everything was working out!

Others were onboarded with me. The organization was staffing up to deploy a national development program. Early on, we regularly met in person to design and develop the program's content. I was getting to know my new peers. We openly shared our thoughts, ideas, and suggestions. Most of us had master's Degrees while others had Ph.D.s. We'd been working together for a few months and one of my peers suggested we write down on Post-it notes something we knew that we could teach other people. Everyone agreed and thought it was a great idea. Inside, I slowly began to panic.

As everyone sat quietly scribbling their talents, skills, and abilities, I sat there. I watched as others filled one note, then another, then another. And I just sat there. I put my pen to the paper, hoping some useful, transferable skill would come to mind, but still – nothing. As my peers began to get up and place their notes on the wall. I still sat there. Then came the intrusive thoughts:

"You're not good enough."
"How did you get hired?"
"Everyone's better than you."
"You can't share something when you know nothing."

I wanted to disappear! I decided at that moment that I was out of my depth. I'd bitten off more than I could chew and was choking!! I managed to jot down a couple of meaningless things, hoping it wouldn't be read aloud or I wouldn't be asked about it. Luckily, we didn't spend too much time on it as I sat there silently mortified. After that day, I thought someone noticed my lack of contribution and it would get back to my executive clients who would be disappointed. They'd learn I wasn't as skilled as they thought and would suggest I be terminated and replaced with a more capable consultant. One shoe had dropped, it was only a matter of time before the other fell, I assumed.

Over the next couple of months, I kept my head down. Doing what was asked of me to the best of my (limited) ability. My clients didn't seem to know how "unqualified" I was...yet. More time passed and my clients started asking me for things. They wanted content on a few familiar topics, so I jumped in and started designing. "Better keep the charade up as long as I can. I'll be 'exposed' soon enough," I thought. After designing, developing, and delivering various leadership development topics, I was surprised I wasn't discovered. I was so focused on meeting my clients' requests, that I forgot how "incompetent" I was.

After about six months, I had a conversation with my manager. I told her that I liked developing new content. My clients were receptive to it, and it was a process that included things I enjoyed: research, sequence, creating activities, etc. She seemed delighted; not concerned or worried but delighted. It slowly began to dawn on me that my executive clients never reached out to her to complain about my work. They seemed quite satisfied.

In that moment the dark cloud over my head for months began to lift. I hadn't been "faking it." I wasn't pretending to be something I wasn't. I'd been meeting, and even, exceeding expectations! Upon reflection, I became angry. I couldn't believe I let one activity convince me I was worthless and not good enough! How could I think that? Then, like a ton of bricks, it hit me. Shit! I'd been dealing with Imposter Syndrome for 6 months (*palm to face*)!

I learned three key things from this experience:

"Comparison is the thief of joy!" – Theodore Roosevelt

It was a crucial mistake for me to compare myself to others based on an activity. That comparison brought on feelings of inferiority and insecurity. Never compare yourself to another! Trust yourself, your knowledge, and your experience. Be curious in the face of challenges instead of judgmental.

"The real you, the inner you, loves and adores you;
but you cut off that power when you think badly of yourself."
– Sue Fitzmaurice

I turned a blind eye to all the great things I had done that got me here. I disconnected myself from the power of ME. Always keep a growth mindset. Find ways to expand on what you know and lean into what you don't to improve over time.

"The only person you are destined to become is the person
you decide to be."
-Ralph Waldo Emerson

Despite how deeply I was affected by imposter syndrome, I kept going. I rediscovered my love for my work, clients, and peers. Once I decided I *was* qualified and competent, I put my strengths to work. You manifest what you believe, so always believe you're capable.

Cassandra Wilson
Coach & Development Consultant
https://www.ascendwithcw.com

Chapter 22
Navigating Deep Disappointments in Life.

"Having a soft heart in a cruel world takes courage not weakness."—Katherine Henson

As I was driving that day, overlooking the beautiful sunset for the last time in a neighborhood that I had called home for over 15 years, I had tears streaming down my face for over 15 minutes. As I parked in my new home, I didn't expect to feel the rush of emotions of relief and joy and sadness at the same time. I wasn't haunted by the good and awful "memories" in every space of the old place anymore, and I was entering my new Single Era in my sanctuary that would be my refuge and safe house for my soul, my new home. Princess, my dog greeted me with such joy that I forgot at least for a couple of minutes the raw reality of my life. I was starting fresh, and hope was activated in my soul.

Navigating this new Single Era at times was torture, but with the women I surrounded myself with it could be straight-up hysterical at times. One evening, I had one of my chicas meet me for dinner at a joint that I usually frequented with "Mr. A." For weeks the owner had been telling me to say hi (I was looking for another word that is not ex-husband) to him, as I would get take out, but this particular friend (my chica), had had enough and blurted to the lady that my "previous tenant" will no longer be coming! From then on the sushi lady hasn't brought it up since, and Mr. A was referred to as the "previous tenant" from then on. I also think she thinks I have women lovers as that is all I bring there.

There are three things that kept my sanity during these challenging times: My faith in God and daily meditation in His word, my board of directors also known as my momma and my closest friends, and my acupuncture and all things holistic—it was my version of the holy trinity.

Grief/sorrow and joy can co-exist in our hearts. I am living proof of this. God is good always and that's a promise I have kept in my heart. He manifested himself in so many ways. I kept telling myself this is just a season.

Grief and loss come in many forms and there is no magic formula that you follow that makes the grief go away or the process of healing move faster. I can tell you that avoiding grief and loss doesn't help, and the inability to mourn can feel crippling. However, when you allow the mourning to be processed in your heart and soul, they have a release rather than holding it in and can be cathartic. It's not easy, but you don't have to do it alone. Releasing the energy of sadness out of your body can be done by feeling the emotion and knowing that it's trying to tell you something. The message isn't harmful; it's just something you aren't used to. It is your body keeping you safe.

Keeping my heart "soft" and not angry and resentful these past couple
of years has been one of my top priorities for my mental and emotional sanity.

Mourning isn't just reserved for when a person dies, it's for when anything dies—a dream, a hope, a plan, a goal, a relationship, an expectation. I had experienced all of that for two years straight.

One day I was reading when I saw this question: how are you watering your "mental garden"?
I loved that concept because at the time I was very lost, so this idea of watering the garden of my mind with good thoughts rather than confusion, exhaustion, anxiety, and the unknown was something I took to heart and it saved my mental and emotional state.

HOPE, don't lose that. I know it's easy to let it go, but it's the lifeline of looking forward to another day when disappointment hits like a ton of bricks.
I can tell you that watering my mental garden with the fruits of the Holy Spirit has led me to feel WHOLE, loved, and fulfilled in ways that I can't describe. I am a girl who trusts God wholeheartedly. My prayer is to keep my heart "soft" and I work on myself every day and know that it's God's provision that supplies all my needs.
I trust God with today.
I trust God with tomorrow.
I trust God with my future.
I simply trust GOD with his timing.

The hard parts of our life journey can be life-altering, but they don't have to be life-ruining.
God's plans will always be more beautiful than our disappointments. Be patient and have a heart of gratitude with your higher being.

Xiomara Escobar
Instagram @thedivawearspink

Chapter 23
HORSE AS HEALER

My career, spanning decades, has been in service as a nurse. Like many of my colleagues in healthcare, we tend to take care of everyone else, neglecting ourselves, and causing burnout. Events in the Spring of 2020 challenged our core.

The morgue of my hospital overflowed during the first week that the coronavirus-19 hit New York City. I walked outside to the loading dock and swung open the heavy metal back doors of a tractor-trailer freezer truck. Inside were dozens of dead bodies stacked on hastily constructed plywood shelving. We were filling freezer trucks with all the people who had succumbed to the virus. The bodies in white body bags looked to me like butterfly cocoons, all clustered together. I prayed that these bodies all grow figurative butterfly wings and fly to whatever destination their faith led them to.

After being a warrioress nurse for about a year and a half, the worst of the pandemic had passed over. Even though things were returning to somewhat normal in the hospital, my thoughts were overwhelming. Feelings of failure and shame related to the death toll of people who had trusted me to save their lives distracted my waking moments and also my dreams. "I've got to get out of here!" I exclaimed out loud.

Later on the plane, out the window, the clouds were fluffy, floating without a care in the world. It was unreal arriving at the destination, the island of Vieques, 4 miles wide and 20 miles long off the east coast of Puerto Rico. The heat was not oppressive but brought a summery warmth to my bones. The island was surrounded by long stretches of uninhabited, pristine beach and balmy crystal-clear turquoise waters of the Caribbean. Palm trees waved their coconuts and fronds in the fresh breeze that smelled of salt and seaweed. Herds of roaming horses made their home in thorny shrubbery and milkweed of nature preserves, vast expanses of clean beige sand peppered with conch shells, and streets lined with tropical-colored cement houses of the small towns.

Unwilling to return to my previous reality, I acquired a job as a horseback trail guide. "Put the new girl on Red,' Jefa said. Red, simply and appropriately named, was a youngish stocky pony with a thick mane and forelock of fuzzy auburn hair. My official job was as a back rider, the guide following behind the line of many clients riding on the tour, watching to make sure everyone was safe. The first day on the job I dismounted after all the riders were through a gate, shut the gate, then attempted to get back on Red. He threw his head up, eyes wide with the whites showing around them, snorting loudly through flared nostrils, and started prancing around in circles. My foot was in the stirrup, but I couldn't get up because I was being dragged around and around. The rest of the group got farther away, riding toward Playa Negra. I was halfway on when Red took off at a gallop, me hanging over his side. We must have been quite a sight; luckily, the tourists were looking forward at the breathtaking view of the beach and not back at me, hanging on for dear life, my horse out of control. Eventually, I remounted and composed myself, and the ride ended on a cliff over the vast ocean. We were engulfed in a vivid pink and purple sunset, like living in an impressionist painting masterpiece.

The next day we were at the gate, and Red became hysterical. Then it occurred to me, he was having anxiety because his safety was connected to being with the herd. Horses are herd animals, and a straggler could, as the horse's DNA will tell him, be eaten by a predator more easily. Red's innate quest for survival was putting him into fight or flight mode as the herd moved away from him. Red was just like me, just trying to survive. "It's OK buddy, I got you." I used soothing voice tones and reassuring pats which worked to quiet him enough for me to get back on.

Herein lies the magic of the horse/human bond. By helping Red through his fits of anxiety, I was able to see clearly and work through my fight-or-flight response. The horse acts as a mirror to our emotions, engaging us in an energy dialogue that transcends vocabulary. A review of current scientific literature reveals that science supports what every horse person knows in their heart: being close to a horse just makes you feel good.

The science behind this is that during the exchange between horse and human, dopamine, serotonin, endorphins, and oxytocin are released. These are the body and the mind's feel-good neurotransmitters and hormones. While communicating with horses and interacting with them, cortisol, the stress hormone, is decreased. Astride of Red, I felt powerful, alive, free, and happy. All that was reduced to noise in my mind and heart had become music again.

One day, in the pasture thousands of orange and black butterflies rose up flying all around us. They were having a love fest; surreal, like something out of a dream. We are all part of the cycle on this tiny Caribbean Island. Egg, caterpillar, cocoon, metamorphosis, butterfly, migration, return to homeland. Birth, Life, Birthing, Transformation, Death. The Taino, the native people of the island, believe that Spirit is everywhere; in the horse and in you. I remembered all the bodies in the makeshift morgue in New York that seemed so far away now. They had looked like cocoons. Now all those horrifying mental images and the thoughts of doom and dread were being replaced with poignant beauty and peaceful easy feelings. Red and I rode through the Monarch rain, and I realized that the prayers I had said for my patients lost in Covid had come true.

My journey to find joy happened somewhat accidentally, through an authentic relationship with a horse. Equine-assisted therapy has become a widespread therapeutic modality with practitioners able to guide anyone through this healing process. Although you don't have to pay for formal therapy to reap the benefits the majestic horse can give you, volunteering at your local horse farm or rescue
could be an option to enrich your life.

Larissa Michelle Pollica
Wellness-lifedoula.com

Chapter 24
Freedom = Happiness?

Happiness is the freedom born of maturity, wisdom, and discipline. Without these, this happiness is delusional and leads to disappointment, heartbreak, and sickness.

I am a spiritual life coach, and I very intentionally set up my coaching practice to afford me the luxury of living anywhere in the world. I am happiest when I am traveling, and having adventures in foreign lands. I am blessed to have built an efficient business system that lets me flourish as a coach and business mentor for women who want this same opportunity.

My lifestyle is the epitome of freedom. I am in control of my time, money, and environment. I get to choose with whom I work.

Am I happy?
You betcha!

But this happiness wasn't just handed to me. The happiness that comes from freedom is hard-won because freedom is an incredibly powerful force that can skyrocket you to joy or catapult you to disaster.

Certainly, I am on the joy trajectory now. But it wasn't always like this. When I was a kid, freedom was disastrous for me.

During the summer of 1978, I stayed with my grandmother, and to keep me out of her hair, she bought me all the food I liked and let me manage it myself. Oh, she always provided me with a healthy, solid breakfast and dinner. But between 10:00 AM and 4:00 PM, I had total freedom over food.

I was SO happy!

My grandmother was an efficient homemaker and for my snacks, I was issued a shelf in the refrigerator and space in the freezer, as well as an entire cabinet in the living room.

The cold stuff consisted of the generic version of Oscar Mayer bologna, Kraft American sliced cheese, Farmer John hot dogs, bacon, sausage, milk, Sunny Delight, and soda pop. My snack cabinet was full of Oreo cookies, Chips Ahoy, Tang, Lay's potato chips, and breakfast cereals like Fruity Pebbles, Cap'n Crunch, Boo-Berry, Count Chocula, Lucky Charms, et cetera. There were also lots of canned foods that I loved like Chef Boy-Ar-Dee Ravioli and Spaghetti-O's. You get the picture, right?

And this is where the trouble began because, as I wrote earlier, deriving true happiness from freedom requires maturity, wisdom, and discipline— none of which I had at age eight.

I think it is safe to say that I was on the opposite end of the maturity spectrum. I was an unhinged ball of emotions because, not only was I contending with an eight-year-old's summertime mind, but I was also contending with the raging hormones that come from an early onset menstrual cycle.

As an eight--year old girl thrust abruptly into womanhood, I could have used some hugs, care, and guidance. But what I got was a box of Kotex sanitary napkins and a day off from my chores.

I didn't know how long my period would last or how much blood would flow. I didn't know how often I would need to change my pad. I had to figure it out as I went along. And how do you hide a giant sanitary napkin under a pair of tight-fitting blue jeans?

All these questions left me in the arms of mystery, which is frustrating for adults and terrifying for children.

The isolation and loneliness I felt was enormous. There was a wide chasm that had formed between me and childhood, and I bridged that gap with eating.

My eating style was simple: eat until it is gone.

Finishing things was a way of controlling and I craved control. So eating a whole box of cookies made me feel complete and whole. Eating a portion of a package of something didn't give me the comfort of knowing that there was more left for later than it did for others. It gave me the anxiety of being *unfinished business*, and that was something that could come back to haunt me.

During the school years that followed that summer, I was a latch-key kid, coming home to be by myself, commanded to essentially shelter-in-place until my mom got home around 9:00 PM.

After a year, though, the circumstances for my mom and I changed, and found myself alone a lot less. But my relationship with food was the same— it was still my source of affection and comfort, always there for me in my time of need.

At the ripe age of 54, I can honestly say that I am truly happy now. It's not just because I am living in Paris, working as a spiritual life coach, writing from my bed looking at the Eiffel Tower. Those things are reflections of the true happiness inside. I have found true happiness through discipline, wisdom, and maturity. The affection I had craved as a hungry child is now being provided by stillness and the embrace of God.

So how can you discover your true happiness that is rooted in freedom? Develop discipline, wisdom, and maturity:

Step 1: Accept that you are not perfect, and that life is meant to be messy and flawed. If your life has no errors, then you're not doing it right.

Step 2: Learn to love your shadows. The pain and trauma from your past have shaped you into a unique human being with a particular flavor. Maybe you're a prickly pear or a tough nut to crack. Rather than hiding your reactions in shame, embrace your wounding as a badge of the human experience.

Step 3: Grow up. If you're still making choices like your 8-year-old self, it's time to take on some adult responsibilities on behalf of yourself. If your issue is food, like mine, or if it's something else— find the healing you need to uplevel the quality of your life.

Step 4: Develop discipline. For me, discipline has truly become the friend who loves me. Many folks find discipline to be abhorrent. But discipline begins with willingness. If you can make yourself willing, the discipline will naturally follow.

Step 5: Commit to willingness. Willingness doesn't require a whole lot of effort; it begins with a simple shift in attitude. Willingness is like a magic portal that lets God's Divine Will have space in your mind and heart.

Step 6: Pray. Get down on your knees and pray for the willingness to put down whatever you're a slave to. God will surely set you free.

Crystal Lynn Bell, Spiritual Life Coach
www.BadassButterfly.com

Chapter 25
"Psychological Safety & Connection"

I'm Trisha—a culture enthusiast, leadership growth catalyst, and dedicated mom and wife. For over 25 years; I've partnered with leaders and teams to unlock their full potential through my work as a consultant, coach, and dynamic facilitator. Whether I'm inspiring a room of hundreds or working closely one-on-one, my mission remains the same: to create environments where people feel safe, valued, and empowered. By prioritizing psychological safety and connection, I've seen firsthand the incredible transformations that can occur within teams and organizations.

Imagine this: You've just started a new job, full of hope and excitement, only to realize within two weeks that you've stepped into a toxic environment. That was me, standing in a conference room, watching a colleague get torn apart by one of the executives. It felt like déjà vu, a flashback to 20 years earlier in the same industry. The discomfort was palpable, and I immediately knew I had to tread carefully.

A month later, it was my turn. The criticism came not in public but behind closed doors. I walked out of that meeting in tears, feeling a profound sense of regret. Fast forward a few months and a peer reported the same toxic behavior. My VP asked what I would do if I were in her position. I answered honestly, suggesting we shouldn't tolerate such negativity on the team. My honesty wasn't appreciated. I was told this individual, despite their behavior, was too valuable to lose. From that moment on, I was marked, and a shift happened.

As the weeks and months passed, the pit in my stomach grew. I left a place where I felt valued and appreciated for a role that quickly turned toxic, and it was a heavy burden. I remember sitting at my desk, staring out the window, and wondering how I could have misjudged the opportunity so badly. The memory of my old colleagues, the camaraderie, and the fulfilling projects haunted me. I'd left on such a high note that this downfall felt crippling; it affected my mental health and well-being.

No matter how great my accomplishments were, there was always a fault to be found. Despite my successes, the focus often shifted to what was missing rather than what was achieved. I accomplished progressive work, praised by presidents of the company's subsidiaries, yet criticized for not divulging my methods—methods no one had asked me about. The scrutiny intensified during a "team-building session." I thought I was having fun, but afterward, I was chastised for not playing politics. In another activity, I symbolized my supportive role as a coach by drawing a safety net, only to be told that safety nets were unnecessary for the team. The constant surveillance and judgment were draining. I felt unappreciated and unwelcome, and I knew I didn't belong.

Years later, I worked with a client who initially wasn't ready to face some deep-seated issues. During a team session, she admitted she didn't trust everyone present, which halted our progress. It was clear we needed a more private, focused approach. I knew that creating a safety net and fostering a meaningful connection were critical for the deep work to begin. We started working together, peeling back layers of assumptions and fears. In one session, I shared a perspective that struck her like a sudden revelation. She paused, reflecting deeply—it was something she had never considered before.

Encouraging her to explore this discomfort, she initially resisted but eventually took the plunge. At our next meeting, she shared her newfound insights and the steps she had taken. Her mindset had shifted dramatically, transforming not just her leadership style but also her readiness to address team dynamics. The breakthrough wasn't just about professional growth but personal transformation.

At the onset of my two-day 'Building Team Dynamics' workshop with her leadership team, she courageously apologized for her previous behavior, acknowledging the mental blocks that had held her back. Her vulnerability created a powerful moment of connection, and she committed to doing meaningful work with them over the two days and beyond. It was a testament to the hard, or rather, heart work we had done together. Her willingness to be open and trust me as her coach was pivotal.

The 'Building Team Dynamics' workshop is one of the most rewarding parts of my work. Designed as an immersive experience, it allows teams to openly evaluate their effectiveness, discuss challenges constructively, and draft new agreements. From the onset, I ensure the tone and atmosphere encourage engagement, openness, and affirmation. This workshop isn't just about team building; it's about transforming how people work together.

If there's one piece of advice, I can leave you with, it's this: To feel safe and connected with others, you must be willing to create that environment. Be the safety net—provide a space where people feel supported and understood, regardless of what others think. This is where deep trust and real transformation begin.

If you're reading this and feeling stuck in a toxic work environment or struggling with your leadership journey, know that you're not alone. Take a moment to reflect on what truly matters to you. Is it integrity, safety, growth, connection, or something else? Whatever it is, let your North Star guide your decisions. I held onto mine and have had no regrets, as time and again, clients have sought out my unique approach. Don't let anyone convince you that what matters to you is unimportant; there will always be people who believe otherwise. Your actions can transform the lives of so many you touch. Embrace the power of creating a safe and connected environment.

Trisha Mason Parsad
www.tmpleadership.com
Leadership Catalyst: Consulting, Coaching, Facilitating, and Speaking Engagements
~Elevating Leadership ~Cultivating Teams ~Igniting Transformation

Chapter 26
"The Mind, Body and Soul Connection"

Have you ever wondered why you are the way you are? Are your thoughts, feelings, and actions a product of your decision-making process or are they driven mostly by outside events in your life?

I believe most of us tend to avoid addressing these questions directly. Often, we are caught in the unsettled flow of life, or worse yet, we exist in "survival mode." This struggle leaves us unable to devote the time and energy that is needed to reflect and resolve our issues. The answer to this dilemma lies in aligning our mind, body, and soul.

Before I became a life coach, I was a hairstylist for 15 years. I am honored to say that I had the amazing opportunity of getting to know many of my clients on a personal level. It was interesting to see continuous similarities between people over the years. I became familiar with different lifestyles, diets, habits, triggers, and quirks. I saw people at their best and at their worst. I got to see how people handled different events and situations that occurred. I learned that emotional pain and suffering can be just as bad or worse than most physical pain.

Sometimes what we think is the worst news, leads to the best news. It was a normal Tuesday morning. I had my routine six month check up at the otolaryngologist office. Everything was fine until I was told that several small tumors were growing inside my ears. I had noticed a decrease in my ability to hear and an increased level of pain but the realization that tumors were present was frightening. Being deaf was not on my calendar! Little did I know that the tumors would turn out to be a blessing in disguise. From a very young age, I had dealt with ear infections, pain, and surgeries. I was told that this was just something I had to deal with. Now, the future looked even more troubling with the prospect of total deafness on the horizon.

Life comes at us fast sometimes; it is not always easy to remain positive. It is, however, easier to return to a positive mindset when we are in alignment. If the mind, soul, and body are in synch the synergistic effect can change everything. When we are aligned, life just flows. Things generally go more smoothly. When hardships arise, we see things from different perspectives, and as a result, we handle our hardships with more grace. Each of us can achieve this kind of balance. We flow in and out of it throughout our entire life, but it is our ability to bring it back into alignment that makes the greatest difference.

The surgery was a success beyond my expectations. The tumors were benign, and the surgeon was able to successfully remove them. Equally important, he was able to repair my inner ear issues. It was at this post surgery stage that I experienced an introspective, healing journey that transcended anything that had happened to me before.

The post op healing was incredibly hard. My ears were filled with packing, I was unable to hear well, and the sound of my heartbeat pounded loudly in my head like a jackhammer. These difficulties, however, served a purpose. By facing my difficulties directly, my coping skills improved and more importantly it served to affirm my belief that adversity itself can be a path to spiritual growth. It forced me to pay attention to my life lessons.

One of the most important lessons for me was what I would have to do if the surgery was unsuccessful. I could not help but wonder how deafness could affect my life and why this was happening to me. These fears gave rise to an epiphany: it is not happening to you; it is happening for you. I needed to employ all of my senses, including my inner self. Once I accepted this premise, miracles began unfolding in my life one after another.

The mind, body, and soul connection is linked through our thoughts and emotions. It can affect our immune system and, over time, define our reality. Once aligned all things are possible.

In today's world, this connection has never been more important and more difficult to achieve. Think of the mind, body, and soul as car. The mind is the engine, it manages all the parts. The body is the body of the car, it goes where it is told and holds it all inside. The soul is you, in the driver's seat. You are the one choosing how to maintain the engine, you are the one giving it fuel, you are the one that tells it where to go. Without the connection to the soul, there is stagnancy. You can be coasting or on autopilot getting yourself mindlessly from point "a" to point" b," but are you aware of where you are going? Awareness builds the connection and allows you to be more in the present moment, consciously choosing to enjoy the journey.

To create better harmony and strengthen your connection with your mind, body, and soul, start wherever you feel the most drawn to.

For the mind, challenge yourself to do something new, a new workout or class, take time to get quiet, meditate or journal. Regularly check in with yourself and prioritize sleep.

For the body, commit to daily movement. Stretch, sweat and breathe. Remember that the food you eat results in how you feel. Simple foods, for simple thoughts.

For the soul, practice cultivating healthy relationships as this helps boost the immune system, reduce anxiety and depression. Spend time alone doing something new or something you enjoy. Practice self-care and self-love. Lastly, keep in mind that when we focus on living our lives in alignment, we will experience peace and tranquility.

Katie Kruse
Life and Wellness Coach and Author
www.coachkatiekruse.com

Chapter 27
"Finding Your Inner Voice and Divine Connection"

Hi, I'm Carolyn, a passionate lover of exploring, learning, and connecting with humanity! As the creator of Warmkins, I help people connect to their inner child and bring comfort and healing hugs to the World. I'm a mother to 3 children, 4 fur babies and am happily married to my best friend.

I was 19 when my father passed away. I would say unexpectedly, though it was only unexpectedly to me. He'd been battling cancer for 7 months, but it was aggressive, and the doctors were not. My parents were private about his prognosis, and I naively leaned on outside reassurances that "modern medicine, faith and prayers" would cure my father.

I was self-absorbed at the time, immersed in my own coming of age, superficial world of dreams and ambitions. I'd been raised in a strong faith-based household, however my youth and innocence had been lost growing up too quickly in the fast-paced L.A. of the 90's. Youth, beauty and connections resulted in alluring and glamorized opportunities surrounding me at every turn, a stark contrast to my conservative upbringing. Those distractions enabled my ungrounding and drifting from the reality of his terminal state.

Upon learning of his passing, I was devastated and rushed home, dropping to my knees and gripping his still warm forearm. A thought entered my mind; this would be the last time ever feeling his physical presence in this life. I was forced to face mortality as a reality. It was a traumatic dose of truth for a teenage girl whose focus was far from pondering the existential meaning of life or end thereof.

While in my state of deep anguish an inner voice beckoned me to quiet my mind. Upon doing so, I heard... "What do you believe? Why do you believe it? What are you going to do about it?"

In my heart, I pondered these 3 existential questions, then sat quietly breathing more slowly now, the tears still wet in my eyes and listened...

Within seconds a conduit opened up, a flood of light, wisdom, understanding and peace downloaded straight into my heart. It came with so much love and conviction that I quickly recognized the familiarity of it...truth, light and love had been inside of me always. The shallow world of smoke and mirrors had drowned out my soul's powerful connection, but In that moment everything changed.

Call it an "a-ha" moment, an awakening to a previously incomprehensible knowing. Losing my father was my a-ha moment, and it awakened my soul to a yearning for even greater understanding and connection with the Divine.

The experience became a catalyst for discovering new dimensions of faith, love and enlightenment. It was a trajectory of spiritual growth and development that would shape the course of my life, setting me on a path of healing and true "Happiness". Amidst the pain of losing my father, the collateral beauty was discovering the gift of my soul's ability to drop into a heart-centered state of communication to Source: a gift that would remain with me for the next 27 years and counting.

My inner voice, what some call intuition or divine guidance, prompted me to make an intentional choice to lean into faith and opt for love over fear that day. I realized that calming the mind and being heart centered is where we can tap into direct communication with Source intelligence and divine energy, enabling a channel of light and wisdom from the Universe. Leaning into higher powers to draw strength became a way of life for me.

I would go on to make drastic changes that year, to clear my energy from the trivial noise of the world and maintain a clearer space for light in my life. Becoming mindful of the heavy and toxic distractions, I eliminated my exposure to those content types in movies, music, news, social circles, etc. - a complete turnabout for me. I became proactive about what my spirit and mind were taking in daily, no longer allowing the world to dictate and control the content or story. I began living with intention and mindfulness.

Leaning into my connection with the Divine and living with love and purpose didn't lessen opportunities, it increased them more than I could have ever imagined and opened doors to an abundant life filled with blessings, adventure and experiences. I was empowered - given help and protection in dangerous scenarios, discernment and clarity in decision making, and resourcefulness and courage when I needed it most. The floodgates opened to creativity and connection, even leading me to envision and develop a product that would bring warmth, comfort and healing hugs to countless people around the world.

If we live in tune to our inner voice, it will increase our confidence and guide us to places we couldn't otherwise begin to comprehend. Our intuition enables us to create, manifest and connect with others on the highest vibrational levels, all leading to greater happiness, knowing that the Universe has our back.

Divine connection on a personal level is like a superpower that each one of us has access to. Once you tap into your superpowers, suddenly problems seem smaller, and more manageable as your focus becomes bigger. You're now standing on an eternal platform where the views are spectacular!

Happiness is knowing we are never alone on this journey and that the Universe conspires for you in perfect timing. Recognize the workings of the Universe at hand in your life and practice listening and connecting with Source to help, guide and comfort you. Remember your true nature and individual worth, and that love, light, and truth already exists inside of you. Trust your higher self and the inner voice that leads with love and the heavens will open to you.
Our minds limit us, our souls are limitless. Quiet the mind and connect your soul to the limitless powers within. This is where true Happiness lives.

Carolyn Rene' Holly
Founder of Warmkins/Author/Creator/Intuitive Soul
www.WarmkinsWorld.com

Chapter28

This is a philosophy I share with billions of other humans. The truth of it was shown to me early in my life. I was nine years old. My family had just moved from the Midwest to Washington State. They bought a house on a small lake, and I thought it was so beautiful. One morning I sat on a log down by the shore, daydreaming, when I sensed a presence. I was compelled to look up and to my right. I saw a disturbance in the air, and I received a message, a thought I knew came from on high. "I have been here before". Before, meaning Earth. Throughout my life there have been other contacts with another level of perception, mostly by clairvoyance and orbs.

"THIS WONDERFUL LIFE"

You were given this great gift of life, this wonderful life, but why THIS life,
why this PARTICULAR life.
"OUR EARTH"

First let us look at life in general. It's a big subject, yes, but we can break it down to manageable parts. First this planet, the most beautiful in the universe, (my guess based on what NASA has shown me). WATER in abundance spawned

NATURE, which seems limitless, and probably is, the right ATMOSPHERE has protected it all, while nourished by the SUN and the MOON.

The universe has a process for balance and growth and that process can be summed up in three words: BIRTH / EVOLVE / TRANSFORM. This is observable by all of us, no need for science PHD's. We are energy and energy never dies it just transforms. The seed / flower / compost. Again, the seed / flower /compost. Ad infinitum.

"SPIRIT"

Humans are part of this process too. We are spirit everlasting and become matter. That is, we are born here on earth, in material form, with one job only. That job is to be born/EVOLVE/transform. This sequence will provide more than one learning opportunity within your lifetime. Let's call them mini rebirths; major obstacles require the same sequence of learning; Rebirth/Evolve/Transform. Your spirit form is "unassigned". That is the spirit form has not status, is genderless, and is non-ethnic, nor does it have any of the other delineations available to our material life here on earth. However, there is a spiritual progress or spiritual loss that stays and accumulates with what has gone on during your "learning" sojourn on earth, (our soul journey).

When you were born to this life it wasn't random, you chose it. Your spirit self, in consultation with your spirit guides, decided when, where and under what circumstances you would be born. A life was chosen to provide learning opportunities via challenges and problems. Whether poor or well off, you will have work to do in perfecting your soul. Luckily, TOOLS are provided in the form of your own personality, aptitudes and character. You also carry forward from the previous life, benefits or negatives earned. Look within, get to know yourself, and discover your tools for coping with those problems and life challenges. Consequently, if you master those lessons, wisdom will have been gained, and progress of the soul achieved. You will have <u>evolved</u>.

The body can now transform back into spirit for a period of rest and contemplation. A new life will be designed to tackle more life lessons. The result will be all life evolved, one person at a time. All people on earth are facing the same conundrum, that of souls evolving. Together as we all grow, we lift up humanity in general and the world in total. Knowing that, how much easier is it to be tolerant and compassionate toward all your fellow man. Don't take life so seriously; we are all in the same leaky boat. If we keep calm and carry on individually, and all of mankind does the same, humanity will be elevated to a higher level. What you say and do and learn adds to the universal unconscious, where all people can avail themselves of it.

"METHUSELAH"

How long will it take and what happens when I am "done"? Methuselah, it is said lived 900 years. I can go along with that; however, nowhere does it state that those 900 years were consecutive. During the eras he lived, life expectancy was a good 60 year average. Hypothetically it took him 15 lifetimes to work himself into a state perfect enough to sit at the right hand of God. I think it's a small boast that it "only" took 15 lifetimes, the average soul I suspect, would take many more than that. (I'm just basing my guess on the usual evening news).

Just consider the sheer number of negative acts we engender ourselves or those that have been perpetrated on us. Then, there are the seven deadly sins, plus the ones pointed out in the Ten Commandments. Add in all of the creative mischief man can invent, which is limitless, and the negatives stretch to infinity. The sheer volume of troubles to confront, whether as an instigator or a victim, would take many lifetimes. In order to learn the way of doing it the "right way" it's easy to see the need of many lifetimes. Try your best to correct your bad characteristics in this life and you won't have to carry them with you into your future lives. (Do yourself a favor).

"YOUR HERE AND NOW"

First, your life is an opportunity not a punishment; every encounter offers a lesson to be learned, an opportunity for Rebirth/Evolve/Transform. Every human's life is to be lived as an individual, and it is not a contest. So confront challenges as just that, a lesson to be learned, and profit by the experience. The valuable confidence gained will let you be free from the judgment and critical scrutiny of lesser-evolved humans. You will be free to pursue happiness and wrestle it from the rest of the world.

Once you realize this you will be able relax and enjoy life. Also, you can avoid those characters selling immortality, you already have it. No cosmetic cream or magic machine is going to make a difference. Be content with whom you are, living the best you can, and save your money for a nice relaxing vacation.

Marlene Berven Stewart
I love feedback! Email me at nustuff12@yahoo.com
Coming Soon;" A Compendium of Irrelevant and Irregular Thought

Chapter 29
The Joyful Journey of Becoming Happy: Embracing the Messiness of Self-Discovery

Leslie Lorraine Wing seeks to uncover the secrets of happiness, sharing her insights and discoveries to inspire positive change and personal growth. Happiness is not merely a destination but a journey to be embraced with open arms and a joyful heart.

Currently, I'm sitting alone on a terrace in the South of France, watching the white sheets I just washed and sprayed with lavender dry. As I reflect on my ongoing journey towards happiness, I feel a surge of gratitude for the experiences that have shaped me. Life has been a rollercoaster of adventures, challenges, and unexpected turns, but amidst it all, I've learned valuable lessons about the pursuit of happiness.

Growing up, I was fortunate to have a loving family and a happy childhood. Yet, somewhere along the way, I found myself yearning for more—more experiences, more adventure, more fulfillment. I immersed myself in books, devouring biographies, and intricate romance novels, always dreaming of the places and people I read about.

I grew up in the Midwest and lived in Indiana, Missouri, Iowa, Oklahoma, and Illinois as we followed my dad's job. I went to three different high schools and attended five universities, which played a big part in shaping me. There's something immensely satisfying about hard work and the sense of accomplishment that comes with creating new friendships and belonging to a new community. In my senior year of university, I did an exchange program in Malta and an internship in Ireland. I met and married a Swede while working in Chicago, and then I moved to Sweden, where I raised three daughters. While moving wasn't something I wanted my daughters to experience, I continued to love international travel and have done so with work and family—I've been to 73 countries and counting.

My studies in journalism allowed me to delve deep into the lives of others, listen to their stories, and share their experiences with the world. It's the red thread that has followed all of my career paths—from radio DJ and corporate communication to a startup founder who has raised VC funding and completed exits. My partner of 25 years and I created a good and successful life.

But life has its twists and turns, and I found myself at a crossroads when I hit rock bottom. Financial abuse stripped away everything I had worked for, leaving me devastated and lost. I cried, I struggled, and I felt like I was drowning in despair. My home became both my sanctuary and my battleground, a place where I sought solace in cleaning and crafting yet couldn't escape the pain of my circumstances and the escalating legal fees. At the time, my knuckles were raw from all the bleach I was using, and my home was acquiring (quite ugly) mosaics I was creating as I unconsciously tried to put my life back together.

In the midst of chaos, I made a decision—I deserved more. It was a simple yet profound realization that sparked a transformation within me. I became determined to reclaim my happiness, to be brave enough to demand more from life.

Finding yourself is no easy feat. It requires courage, resilience, and a willingness to embrace change. While I could no longer afford the first-class trappings my children and ex-husband continued to have as their norm, I became a magnet for positive energy and cost-free simple pleasures, welcoming every opportunity for growth and self-discovery. I learned the importance of self-care, of allowing myself to rest and recharge, even amidst the chaos. Sacrifice and selflessness became sources of joy, as I found fulfillment in acts of kindness and the simple pleasure of a clean home. I began to take in some tenants to help me during this difficult time. I found out I was good at that and was awarded super host status with 100% 5-star ratings.

I did daily exercise and heat augmentation, which, in my case, was taking a sauna and then plunging into ice water. Pushing myself out of my comfort zone became a mantra, propelling me forward on my journey toward happiness. During that opening of my mind, I challenged myself to try new things, explore new environments, and visualize the future I desired. I met new friends through these hobbies and spoke of my dreams, and like magic, they started to become opportunities even though I was facing a difficult economic time.

As I reflect on my journey, I'm reminded of a calling, an inexplicable urge to explore the far reaches of the world, to immerse myself in unfamiliar landscapes and cultures. During this process, I've decided to work in places of my dreams. From the dark winters and Nordic lights above the Arctic Circle in Jokkmokk, Sweden, to the sun-drenched terraces of Southern France, I've sought solace and inspiration in the beauty of nature and the kindness of strangers. I'm working at BnBs in exchange for room and board and the chance to be included in their families' real daily lives. My hands once again smell of bleach, and I'm so happy to be part of making guests happy. I've helped reindeer herders and eco-wine producers with growing their businesses. That, along with the amazing nature experiences and slow-paced travel opportunities, are incredible. I feel thankful that I am able to do this.

I'm looking for where I can create my next life chapter. And though I haven't found my forever home yet, I'm content with the knowledge that I'm one step closer to finding it. With each new experience and each new adventure, I'm crafting a life filled with joy, purpose, and love.

To anyone embarking on their own journey towards happiness, I offer these words of encouragement: embrace the messiness, lean into the uncertainty, and trust in the power of your resilience. The path to happiness may be winding and unpredictable, but the happiness on the route to the destination is worth every step of the journey.

Here are strategies that are working for me and might be helpful for you:

1. **Be brave enough to demand more.**
   - Face Your Fears: Embrace discomfort and confront your fears head-on.
   - Heal Alone but Seek Support: Surround yourself with people who lift you and support your journey.
   - Take Risks: Don't be afraid to take calculated risks in pursuit of your happiness.
2. **Work for more.**
   - Set Goals: Identify what you want to achieve and create a plan to reach those goals.
   - Prioritize Self-Care: Make self-care a non-negotiable part of your routine.
   - Stay Persistent: Remember that progress takes time and effort. Stay committed to your goals, even when faced with setbacks.

Leslie Lorraine Wing *Author, entrepreneur, and explorer*
https://www.instagram.com/wing_lorraine

Chapter 30
Happiness: It's Easier Than You Think!

The Dinner Party

As the Executive Producer and Host of *ACIM.TV*, a spiritual lecturer on *A Course in Miracles*, and an Instructor for the National Guild of Hypnotists, spiritual development is my primary focus. I have taught everything from EFT with the Source Technique™, Advanced Hypnosis and Regression to Life Coaching and Sound Therapy. But life wasn't always this way.

My spiritual journey escalated after a painful divorce and unexpected layoff from my position as Chief Financial Officer. During my 22 years in finance, I relied on numbers, forecasts, and accounting principles to reach my conclusions; yet it was divine intervention at a dinner party that nudged me in a new direction, changing my life forever.

After my divorce, I felt a heavy weight on my chest, almost suffocating me. No matter what I tried, I couldn't make that feeling go away. My old habit of solving problems myself was leading nowhere, and I was exhausted. It finally occurred to me that maybe God could help. Out of desperation, I asked God to help me find the answer.

Within twenty-four hours, I was invited to a dinner party. During some friendly banter, this nice couple offered to muscle test me on the simple statement, "I am worthy of a happy life." Muscle testing is a quick way of using your body to determine what you believe at a deep, subconscious level. This test would determine if I actually *believed* that I was worthy of a happy life, so I eagerly agreed. The nice couple invited me into a side room and instructed me to hold my arm out while repeating, "I am worthy of a happy life," keeping my arm strong while they gently pushed it towards the floor. I was sure that I would pass the test with flying colors, as I repeated the phrase. But my arm fell limp like a wet noodle. "Oh my gosh!" I spoke. "Test me again!" They did as I asked, but once again, down she went. To confirm the results, they reversed the statement, asking me to say, "I am not worthy of a happy life." To my shock, my arm locked in place with superhuman strength: and in that moment, I knew something was very wrong. My inside wires had been crossed. Worse yet, it appeared *I* was the dirty double-crosser! Everything began to make sense. No wonder I always felt like I was swimming upstream in life. How could anything go well for me, when my own subconscious mind was sabotaging my success? Failing the test shocked me, yet the experience lit a fire within me to get things turned around—FAST!

The Turnaround

I had already learned that trying to solve this problem myself was the last thing I should do, so I went to God first. I was guided to invite the couple from the dinner party to my home for a healing session. They showed me a healing tool called E.F.T. (Emotional Freedom Techniques). Within minutes, the weight on my chest was nearly gone, and I was testing positive for feeling worthy of a happy life. Hallelujah!

It felt like God had put me on a roller coaster of learning and I was on for the ride! I had never experienced such rapid healing before, which prompted me to dive headfirst into learning this technique and ultimately become an E.F.T. Master Instructor. The journey didn't stop there: E.F.T. is wonderful for bringing down the charge from emotional pain, but it was *A*

Course in Miracles which taught me that all healing is of the mind: the mind must be healed for lasting healing to be accomplished. So, I turned my focus towards the mind and asked God to show me what had been driving me to sabotage my own life.

My deep dive into the subconscious mind helped me identify my hidden beliefs (the root cause of my challenges). Through training in *A Course in Miracles*, hypnotherapy, past-life regression, sound therapy, voice analysis, guided visualization, and life coaching, my sabotaging beliefs were neutralized and reset, so I could confidently thrive and live a happy life. Ultimately, I combined E.F.T. with the principles of *A Course in Miracles* and formed my own proprietary method called E.F.T. Prayer Tapping™ for extraordinary healing.

Forgive, Refuse, and Choose Again

After almost three decades of prayer, listening, deep study, and practice, one of the most important tips I can share with you is this: you are not alone. God loves you completely and is always eager to help you. He created you to be happy and to know His love and support in every aspect of your life.

I would like to share three simple steps with you that will help you find your way to happiness—the kind that does not grow dim or disappear. Whenever you are feeling unhappy, and you would like to move towards a happier outcome, I hope you will give these steps a try:

1) Forgive – Take a moment to forgive whatever and whoever you are judging (yourself, others, God, and even inanimate objects). For instance, if you stub your toe on a coffee table, forgive the coffee table! Say to yourself: "I wholly forgive _____ for _____. I want peace instead of pain, and a happy outcome instead of anger and judgment."

2) Refuse – Next, it's time to refuse to validate your old, hidden beliefs. Say to yourself, "I refuse to revalidate

my old belief(s) that I am not safe, loved, supported, healthy, financially secure (or whatever you believe you are missing)." Follow this statement with, "I am not defined by my past. I am defined by God and entitled to a happy life."

3) Choose Again – You are now ready to make a new choice and replace the old, sabotaging beliefs blocking your happiness. The moment you do this, your Higher Consciousness will intervene, reinforcing every effort you make. You can say to yourself, "My goal is the highest level of peace for everyone involved." Or you can try, "Thank You, God, for deciding for me about everything." Or, you can even say, "I choose the highest, happiest, and most remarkable outcome for everyone involved" or some combination of all three statements.

Once you have *forgiven* your reasons for pain and suffering, by no longer needing to be right about anyone's guilt, and *refused* to reinvest in old, sabotaging beliefs or judgments against yourself... You are now ready to choose again, being aligned and receptive to God's love, guidance and happy plan for your life—and a happy outcome is assured!

Robin Duncan
Spiritual Teacher & Mentor
www.robinduncan.com

Thank you for being a part of this book! Just you picking this book up and reading it is a big part of your commitment to happiness. By studying it, taking notes, and really absorbing the material, you gain tools and knowledge on healing your mind, body and soul. Watch your life change as you apply the ideas that resonate with you. Jim Rohn always said, "work harder on yourself than you do on your job." You can now decide to be the happiest, healthiest, most peaceful, unique, creative, fun, and inspiring version of yourself. Choose to heal the issues, work on the inside and the outside. Be the light! Use this as your go to guide to inspire happiness.

To conclude, I leave you with the reminder that you are perfect in your own unique way. The pressures of living the American dream often encourage us to be perfect. We often feel we need to meet extremely high standards, look like celebrities, and never make mistakes. If we do not meet these crazy criteria, we feel unworthy, not enough or even unloved. This has to do with the belief or definition of perfect that has been ingrained in our minds. Is this a fact? Of course not. The true definition of perfect is actually having all the required or desirable elements, qualities, or characteristics as good as it is possible to be. This can be interpreted so many ways. We have the power to decide how to look at and apply this. We can stop punishing ourselves with these unattainable ideals and look at what our authentic perfection can be.

We are all born in utter perfection; pure, wonderful and unique. Through the years, baggage and layers form as a result of beliefs, choices, communication and lifestyle.
This creates layers and blocks that prevent us from being who we truly are. We begin living and seeing and communicating through these painful layers, which creates confusion, problems and low energy, and is the illusion that we are not perfect. The key is to begin working on getting back to that authentic self.

Here are six tips and tools to get you there faster and always love, live and experience utter perfection.

1. Peel away the layers to get to the true you. This may be difficult through the process, but so worthwhile. Many people need a coach or therapist to help them with this. Taking the experiences, emotions, pain, and anything negative that is blocking your truest self, and getting to that breakthrough, analyzing it, letting it go and keeping the wisdom is key. This will leave you with the happy you, the bold, strong, brave and non-judgmental you.

2. Embracing your uniqueness.
We all have very special or unusual qualities. Sometimes we feel that they are too silly or different to let them out. By owning these unique gifts, we present ourselves as standing out from the crowd, as our perfection. Think of an interesting teacher you've had, a musician, or even a family member. Maybe their laugh, their quick wit, or even their hula hooping skills make them unique. You remember them this way, and they own who they are. You can do this too. Think of the qualities you have and begin to celebrate them.

3. Radiating out who you truly are deep inside. Create a list of at least ten things you love about you. Now, decide which qualities you would like to radiate out every day. Would you like to radiate out love, living by example, enthusiasm, compassion, and kindness? Decide each morning to do so and go for it. This way you are in tune with who you want to be.

4. Feel happy and fulfilled. Train your brain to be extra happy by telling yourself regularly that things, people, experiences and you yourself, make you happy. Walk by flowers and tell yourself that they make you happy. Experience a sunset and remind your brain that this is joy. Spend time with a best friend and remind your mind that this is fulfilling. The more you train your brain that your life is happy and fulfilling, your life will become so.

5. Create your dreams. Create your own opportunities and jump into them. Whatever you want in life, find out how to go about getting it. You can ask for help, start researching, take action and move in big and small steps toward what you wish for.

6. Touch others' lives. We all have a responsibility to live by example. This means becoming the best true us possible. When we become our authentic selves, we feel happier and can touch someone's life by just giving them a sentence of advice, smiling or even helping them out.

Remember that true perfection is when you find your authentic self, know who you truly are and let it out, and feel amazing in your own skin. You can define perfection as your own special ideal that is the real you. How wonderful to let that out to the world and not have to be like anyone else. You are on your way to being even happier from now and moving forward. Congratulations! Love and hugs, Kim Somers Egelsee.

To find out more about upcoming events, projects or how to work with me go to
www.kimlifecoach.com or www.higvibesoulsisters.com
or follow me on Instagram at @kimifecoach

Purchase my books; "Getting Your Life to a Ten Plus" and "Living the Ten Plus Life" on Amazon.com or Barnes & Noble.com.

Made in the USA
Las Vegas, NV
23 November 2024

12487267R00079